ENDORSEMENTS

"I don't think I have ever read a more timely book than this! It is a *now* word for a troubled church. It will settle you, strengthen you, and stabilize your faith. *Fierce Peace: Living in a Peace That's Stronger Than the Storm* is just what the doctor ordered for our nations. How we need a fresh infusion of the Fierce Peace of God!

My, my; read this, devour it, and rest your heart in the truths it presents. This is not fluff, it is full of delicious fruit for the lovers of God. Rest your heart today in the divine peace that is so much stronger than the storm you're going through. Thank you, Andrew Hopkins, for this book!"

Brian Simmons
Passion & Fire Ministries
Lead translator of *The Passion Translation*

"Take your time with this one—the writing is crisp, coherent, and clear. Andrew speaks from the authority of his own journey. You're going to learn how to apprehend peace from someone who learned from experience. During a global pandemic of anxiety, thank you for going before us, Andrew, and showing us the way forward."

Bob Sorge
Author of *Secrets of the Secret Place*

"Anxiety is likely at an all-time high right now on earth. It's coming at us full force from any screen we look at. That means God gave Andrew this book at just the right time, since these pages hit back with an even greater force: "shalom." Shalom has been defined as 'the Spirit that destroys chaos,' and this book will not help you tame, manage, or control anxiety; it will destroy it. Enjoy!"

Seth Dahl
Author of *Curing Worry God's Way* and
Raising Spirit-Led Kids

"Since 2020, it has felt like the world has gone crazy—and people have gotten caught up in the chaos. The result is that many are living with an unending sense of anxiety, worry, fear, and confusion.

As a pastor of a large church in Southern California, I have watched as literally thousands of people in the church I lead have been ravaged by the division, dissension, strife, fear, and polarization in our world over the last two years. In *Fierce Peace*, Andrew Hopkins gives the solution from the heart of God: shalom.

I see this book as a tool that the people I love and lead can engage with to regain what has been ripped from them—and I'm so glad it has been written!

Andrew's instruction is thorough—but his goal isn't just to dispense information about peace. His aim is to ensure that you are engaged in a personal process of transformation that will lead you to be fully activated in pursuing and experiencing peace. This book is going to take you on a trip through revelation—right into a workshop where the shalom of Jesus is going to be formed more fully in you!

If you are struggling with the way the chaos in the world has affected you, go on the journey back to peace with this book. *Fierce Peace* is going to realign your spirit so you can step into shalom!"

John V. Hansen

Lead Pastor, Centerpoint Church, Murrieta, CA

www.mycenterpoint.tv

Founder, Filled to Flow Ministries www.filledtoflow.com

FIERCE PEACE

LIVING IN A PEACE THAT'S STRONGER THAN THE STORM

ANDREW HOPKINS

Published by Breaker Ministries
www.breakerministries.com

Cover design by semnitz™ and Andrew Hopkins
Interior design by Sally Hanan of Inksnatcher.com

ISBN print: 978-1-7351430-2-6
ISBN eBook: 978-1-7351430-3-3

CONTENTS

To my sweet wife, Rochelle. You embody the fierce peace of God and are a constant anchor through the storms.

I love you, Huns.

INTRODUCTION

THE WARRING PRINCE OF PEACE

The past season the world has undergone (and is still experiencing) has given us all the opportunity to experience stress, fear, and anxiety. But it has also provided the opportunity to experience the peace of God that is stronger than the shaking. Specifically, this, the anchor text for this book:

> Be anxious for nothing, but in everything by prayer and supplication, with thanksgiving, let your requests be made known to God; and the peace of God, which surpasses all understanding, will guard your hearts and minds through Christ Jesus.
>
> —Philippians 4:6–7

In August of 2020, five months into the worldwide pandemic, I had an encounter with the Prince of Peace.

I was in prayer when, in a vision, a Man clothed in samurai armor appeared. He held out His sword to me and touched my chest with it. I usually walk when I pray, so when He did that, I stopped in my tracks.

I instinctively began to lean back until I was lying on the ground, His sword still touching my chest as it followed me down to the ground. The sword said "peace" on it.

And then He spoke to me saying, "Don't ever call My peace passive."

He turned around, with sword drawn, and stood guard over me. I rested while He guarded.

I realized that I had just experienced Philippians 4:6–7.

There's more to this encounter, which I'll unpack in Chapter 5, but one thing I want to point out from the start is the fierce nature of peace.

Jesus is called the "Prince of Peace" in Isaiah 9:6. A closer look at the Hebrew word for "prince" shows that a more complete translation would render as "warring prince." No wonder why the Lord came to me in armor. He's the *Warring* Prince of Peace!

What is He warring against? The enemies of your peace. He wants to stand guard over your heart and mind to prevent the hostile invasions of fear, anxiety, guilt, shame, unrest, chaos, and the like. Chances are if you're reading this book, you've had your fair share of battles with those enemies.

Like all things in the kingdom, this peace doesn't come from stress and striving—it comes from faith and yielding. Although peace brings rest, it's not passive in nature. It's an active Person who fights on your behalf.

Peace is a Fierce Protector.

In this book, we're going to take a closer look at what peace is, what it's not, how Jesus demonstrated it, and learn practical ways to access God's peace.

It is, after all, *God's* peace.

It's who He is; it's in His nature. It's His atmosphere.

He is unshaken by the storms, still full of compassion and understanding, and He's calling you higher into His realm and His ways.

Regardless of the storms you may be facing, you can still walk in peace. What's going on inside of you is more important than what's going on around you.

The goal of this book is that you would learn to walk in a peace that is *stronger than the storm.*

— 1 —

Two Realities

"I have told you these things, so that in me you may have peace. In this world you will have trouble. But take heart! I have overcome the world."

—John 16:33 (NIV)

It was the middle of 2008, and I had been fighting anxiety attacks most of the year. Not that there's any good time to experience an anxiety attack, but they'd come at the worst times to have them—while I was leading worship, while I was on a date with my then girlfriend, now wife, or while hanging out with friends.

I remember one day that year, as I was waking up in the morning, a wave of anxiety came over me. These attacks would usually come with bewildered thoughts, a lack of clarity, and a racing heartbeat.

All I knew to do was to grab my Bible and get the Word of God.

I read Isaiah 26:3 (NIV) over and over:

> "You will keep in perfect peace
> those whose minds are steadfast,
> because they trust in you."

Within moments the anxiety subsided and rest came.

From that year up to this present day, I've learned much about overcoming fear and walking in peace. You might be fighting anxiety attacks like I was, or you might have areas where the spirit of fear is trying to dominate your thought life. The truth is, His promise of peace works no matter where you find yourself.

Jesus told His disciples that there are two realities that we live in: trouble and peace. In this world, trouble. In Him, peace. We can live in peace even in the midst of trouble.[1]

Here Comes Trouble

The Greek word for trouble in John 16:33 is *thlipsis.* It means a pressing or pressure. It metaphorically means oppression, affliction, tribulation, or distress.[2] Now I'm sure no one has ever held onto this part of the verse as a promise to believe God for...but a quick look at the world around will notify us that our world today is no stranger to what Jesus said would happen.

According to studies, stress causes over 50 percent of diseases in America. The global pandemic has obviously been a source of pressure for many; not to mention the U.S. elections of 2020, the political rage that has swept over the nation, and the racial tensions we've faced.

Then there's the personal issues many have faced in the last year (which, for some, are related to the above-mentioned pressures). People have lost jobs, lost loved ones, and even gone so far as to take their own lives. Mental health has risen as a forefront issue for many.

The pressure has become unbearable for some.

For others, the lack of peace isn't as dominating, but it still has its ill-effects. It's the insecurity that drives decisions, the worry that keeps the mind running, or the unease that brings hypersensitivity. It may be the discouragement that produces apathy, the detachment that puts you on autopilot, or the shame that kills your confidence and joy.

The trouble, when mis-handled, can turn the pressures into anxiety. The challenge we face is learning how to live in peace even while trouble may remain.

The risk we run in not confronting our fears and learning to walk in peace is that we become comfortable in anxiety. It becomes a way of life for us instead of an enemy of life. It falls under the category of "steal, kill, and destroy" and according to Jesus, it's a thief (John 10:10). It's time to deal with the thief!

God's Heart

Quite possibly one of the top three most popular Bible verses is Jeremiah 29:11 (with John 3:16 and Proverbs 3:5–6 topping that list).

> "'For I know the plans I have for you,' declares the Lord, 'plans to prosper you and not to harm you, plans to give you hope and a future'" (NIV).

> "For I know the thoughts that I think toward you, says the Lord, thoughts of peace and not of evil, to give you a future and a hope."

The thoughts or plans of the Lord for you are of *peace*! The Hebrew word for peace is *shalom.* We'll look at this word more in depth in the next couple chapters, but for now, *shalom* means: peace, completeness, soundness, welfare, health, prosperity, tranquility, absence of agitation, and contentment.[3]

This is God's intention for you.

Jesus said it like this: "Peace I leave with you, My peace I give to you; not as the world gives do I give to you. Let not your heart be troubled, neither let it be afraid" (John 14:27). "In Me you may have peace" (John 16:33).

God wants you to live in peace. Jesus said that in Him is peace. He wouldn't say it if it wasn't possible. It's possible to live in peace, even if trouble is all around.

Peace is rooted in a Person, not a circumstance.

A brief survey of Psalm 2 shows us the posture of a world in turmoil in contrast to the posture of our God. The nations are raging and the kings of earth are coming against the Lord...and God is sitting on His throne *laughing*.

He is completely unmoved, unshaken, and unintimidated by the trouble. Peace is not the absence of trouble, but rather regardless of trouble.

BORN INTO HOSTILITY

I love the Christmas season. It's always painted the picture of warm family time, joyful gatherings, lots of good food, presents, and fun. But the over-commercialization of the holiday can deter us from the reality of the world's condition on the first Christmas.

Jesus was born into a hostile world.

Although the lyric "all is calm, all I bright" may have described the beauty of beholding the Son of God coming into the world, the world was not very welcoming. And to be sure, He was the "thrill of hope" that causes a weary world to rejoice, but not everyone recognized Him!

In other words, Jesus came into a real world with real issues just like we have.

Because of the lack of clarity around Mary's supernatural pregnancy, she could have been ostracized and even stoned to death for what some could have misinterpreted as illegitimate. That's dicey considering she was carrying the Answer to world's problems! Then once the Child was born, there was no room for them in the Inn, and eventually they had to flee to Egypt to escape the death threat of Herod.

As Jesus ministered later on in life, people tried to kill him multiple times and even called Him the devil. His disciples didn't always get along and His nation was overruled by the Romans. A people, who, after considering what they did to Jesus in flogging, mocking, and crucifixion, I'd say were pretty hostile.

Through all of this, Jesus stayed in peace. Trouble was definitely all around, but peace was abounding in Him.

The Warring Prince of Peace

The title "Prince of Peace" comes from Isaiah's prophecy of the Messiah—

> For to us a child is born,
> to us a son is given,
> and the government will be on his shoulders.

And he will be called
Wonderful Counselor, Mighty God,
Everlasting Father, Prince of Peace.

—Isaiah 9:6 NIV

What's more is—a closer look at all of those prophetic titles for Jesus speak of a king who fights with military strength. Summarizing what the NET Bible notes say, we see this:

Wonderful Counselor (or Extraordinary Strategist) – refers to the king's ability to devise military strategy.

Mighty God – the Hebrew word for "mighty" implies a warrior.

Everlasting Father – this title pictures the king as the protector of his people.

Prince of Peace – he establishes peace through military strength. His people experience safety and prosperity because their invincible king destroys their enemies.[4]

Clearly this King would not be passive. Later in his book, Isaiah would further say that the Lord would

"put on righteousness as a breastplate,
And a helmet of salvation on His head;
He put on the garments of vengeance for clothing,
And was clad with zeal as a cloak."

—Isaiah 59:17

The dictionary defines peace as the "normal, nonwarring condition of a nation, group of nations, or the world."[5] Yet, Jesus is the Warring Prince of Peace; He establishes peace through war. Jews of Jesus' day would've interpreted that as the Messiah overtaking Rome and establishing Israel's kingdom again like kings in the past did. But His fight wasn't with flesh and blood. It was much deeper than that.

He wasn't there to defeat Rome. He was there defeating our sin and the works of the enemy.

John later said it like this: "For this purpose the Son of God was manifested, that He might destroy the works of the devil" (1 John 3:8).

Jesus came to defeat the enemies of our peace.

Israel would've loved it if Jesus came and destroyed the Roman oppression and took away their outward trouble. Just like them, we would love for Jesus to come and take away our trying circumstances (because we think they're the cause of our lack of peace). Sometimes He does.

But one thing He did make available for us is that come good times or bad times, we can have peace regardless. Jesus didn't come to change your circumstance as much as He came to change your heart.

He Paid for Our Peace

One verse you're going to want to meditate on throughout reading this book is Isaiah 53:5—

> "But He was wounded for our transgressions,
> He was bruised for our iniquities;

> The chastisement for our peace was upon Him,
> And by His stripes we are healed."

I love how Isaiah said, "The chastisement for *our* peace was upon Him."

It belongs to us. It's *ours.*

Check out the way these other translations translated that part of the verse:

> "The punishment that brought us peace was on him" (NIV).
>
> "He endured the punishment that made us completely whole" (TPT).
>
> "He endured the breaking that made us whole" (Voice).

Jesus was beaten and broken to give us *peace.*

In other words, Jesus believed that peace was important enough for us to have that He gave His life for it. God sent Jesus because He wanted to make us whole. The gospel isn't about going to heaven one day; it's about whether we're in heaven or on earth, we'd be whole.

Jesus gave His life for us so that we'd have peace regardless of the circumstances.

A Prayer to Get You There

Father, thank You that You want me to be in peace. I open up my heart to the truth that You want me in peace. I believe Jesus died on the cross to give me peace. Come Holy Spirit and release the peace of God in me. No matter what my circumstances are, I can rest in You.

— 2 —

More than Hippie Vibes

Gideon built an altar there to the Lord,
and called it The-Lord-Is-Peace.
—Judges 6:24

Don't judge me...but...anyone else ever watch the movie *Miss Congeniality*? It's a little old...and some may say it's a chick flick...whatever. In it, Sandra Bullock plays an undercover cop running for Miss America. After many of the contestants announce their stereotypical desire for world peace, she has her conversation with the host—

"What is the one most important thing our society needs?"

"That would be harsher punishment for parole violators, Stan..."

crickets

"...and world peace."

audience cheers

The world has a definition of peace. But it seems it's based mostly on circumstances. As mentioned in the last chapter, the dictionary defines peace as: "the normal, nonwarring condition of a nation, group of nations, or the world."[6] As we've seen, the peace we're talking about has much more to do with what's going on *inside* of you rather than *around* you.

This chapter will take a closer look at peace—according to God.

WHAT PEACE IS NOT

It'd be helpful to know what we're *not* talking about when referring to peace. We're not talking about:

- a passivity that turns you into a doormat and allows everyone to walk all over you in the name of "keeping the peace"
- people pleasing, i.e., trying to make everyone happy
- indulging in the desires of the flesh to make you feel better temporarily
- perfect or ideal outward circumstances (although I appreciate that)
- political correctness
- emptying yourself, i.e., New Age vibes
- hippie vibes and tie-dye t-shirts

Peace can be the absence of war; but it can also be regardless of war.

It's not found in humanism. Oxford Languages defines humanism as an outlook or system of thought attaching prime importance to human rather than divine or supernatural matters.[7] Dictionary.com says that humanism often rejects the importance of belief in God.[8]

We need something outside of ourselves to help! We don't want to be limited to what only humans can do when it comes to peace. We need God.

Peace is putting things back into God's order, into His original design.

My wife and I have two young boys, and we get what chaos can feel like. In those chaotic moments, the kids need discipline and order (of course, we have our fair share of chaotic fun as well). But all parents know that peace and quiet in the house is a wonderful thing.

Peace comes when the house is put in order.

Value Peace

I come from a passionate, charismatic background. Which means we've got the wildest manifestations on a regular basis. And to be clear, I love it. I wouldn't have it any other way.

But if there's a weakness we'd be tempted in, it'd be to not value the manifestation of peace. While we'd definitely broadcast the testimony of someone getting up out of a wheelchair or the electric atmosphere of the high praise—we're not always celebrating the restful tranquility that came over someone.

It's as if it's seen as a lesser manifestation. While I still get super excited about those other manifestations, I can't apathetically walk past the peace of God. The problem is, if we don't value peace, we won't pursue it like we should. Scripture says if we want to love our lives and see good days, one of the things we need to do is pursue peace (see Ps. 34:14, 1 Pet. 3:11).

Truth is, peace is one third of the kingdom of God! (Romans 14:17). It's evidence that the kingdom of God has come—just as much as healing and deliverance is (see

Luke 10:9, 11:20). It made the list of the fruit of the Holy Spirit (Gal. 5:22).

Peace Is Wholeness

Let's revisit the definition of the Hebrew word *shalom.* It means peace, completeness, soundness, welfare, health, prosperity, tranquility, and contentment. It means wholeness. Wholeness has been described as nothing missing, nothing broken.

Think on that for moment: *nothing missing, nothing broken.*

Jesus endured the punishment to make us whole. To give us a life where we have nothing missing and nothing broken. God loved us so much that He wanted to make us *whole.* Ultimately, peace with God is where all of this starts (which we'll get into in the next chapter).

Much of the stress and anxiety in our lives comes from our own brokenness. Our areas of brokenness act as filters through which we can misinterpret life—and because of that, anxiety comes creeping in.

For example, we'll take words of loving correction as identity statements because we still find our identity in our performance and not in Christ. So, when someone points out a mistake we made, it really hurts us and sets us back—when, in fact, it was supposed to help us get better. In short, if you fail, it doesn't make you a failure. You just got an education. A heart at peace wouldn't be shaken by critique, it would be edified.

Past wounds and traumas can become filters that distort our perception of reality. Jesus wants to come into those areas and bring healing and wholeness. He wants to empower you to forgive those who've hurt you, let go of the past, and walk with a fortified sense of your identity in Christ.

Wholeness is restoring the image of God in us where it's been marred. You were destined to become like Jesus (Rom. 8:29).

We could write volumes to help us explore the riches of who we are in Christ: The truth that you're forgiven, accepted, loved, valued, and chosen before the foundation of the world; that you've been called with a holy calling, sealed with the Holy Spirit, anointed with power, and given the authority of Christ; that you're a part of a global family of believers, your citizenship is in heaven, and you're empowered to bring heaven to earth.

Insecurities that lead to anxiety are swallowed up in the love of God. Rejection that negatively impacts your approach to life is overcome by the acceptance of Christ. Pain and trauma that scarred your heart is healed by the oil and wine of the Spirit.

WHO'S TELLING THE STORY?

The question is, what voice is telling your story? Who holds the narrative?

Whoever holds the narrative in your life holds your perception of reality. And out of that—your functionality, and ultimately your destiny.

Remember the story of Adam and Eve? Their perception of reality became distorted because they let someone other than God tell the story. Which, by the way, is the reason the tree of the knowledge of good and evil was not good for them to eat of; it allowed them to receive information outside of their relationship with God (I believe it's the root of humanism). They had the choice to let God, the Creator of everything, be their world view, or another voice.

I love what Bill Johnson says: "Anything outside of the Presence is subject to distortion."

Surrendering the narration of their lives to another voice affected how they saw God, how they saw themselves, and how they saw their circumstances. It will do the same in our lives:

1. Our perception of God

In Genesis 3, the serpent painted a negative picture of God by, in essence, saying to Eve that God was holding out on them. He painted a deceptive "less than good" picture of who God is. As a result, the first humans disobeyed God and their perception became distorted. They ran and hid from Him because fear began to tell the story.

A.W. Tozer said, "What comes into our minds when we think about God is the most important thing about us...We tend by a secret law of the soul to move toward our mental image of God."[9]

Instead of the inconsistencies of our emotions and distorted perceptions, we need the truth of God's Word to inform our beliefs about who He is. His truth is the anchor in the storm.

He is good.

He is love.

He is kind.

2. Our perception of ourselves

One of the most powerful questions God ever asked was, "Who told you that you were naked?" (Gen. 3:11) In other words, God asked Adam, "Who is telling your story? Who gave you your self-perception?"

"Who told you that you were ______________?" (you fill in the blank)

Where did we get our perception of who we are?

Follow that up with, is that even true? Does what I believe about myself line up with what God says about me?

Forgiven.

Accepted.

Called.

Anointed.

Empowered.

3. Our perception of our circumstances

Fear was driving the narrative in Adam and Eve's lives...and it's still trying to drive the narrative for many today.

Who's telling the story in your circumstances? Fear cripples and distorts but hope strengthens and invigorates. Biblical hope is an eager expectation that good is coming your way.

During that battling season of 2008, I remember hearing Joel Osteen say this: "The good thing about seasons is that they have a beginning and an end. That means wherever you are in life, you're not there forever." It was like he handed me the key of hope. I knew that I wasn't going to be stuck where I was forever; there was an end to this thing.

It's the key of hope. It unlocks the sense of possibility that life will change. It *will* get better. If you don't believe it'll get better, your mindset can perpetuate depression. Hope breaks the sense of being stuck. Hope unlocks faith. Hope is like a breaker anointing that breaks open the way to see what is possible.

When fighting anxiety and depression, hope is paramount. You need to know that there is hope for freedom, hope for change, and you're not stuck where you are forever.

Our God is the God of hope. Let Him be the narrator of your circumstances.

THE GOD OF PEACE

> "The God of peace will crush Satan under your feet shortly" (Romans 16:20).
>
> "Unto us a Son is given...And His name will be called...Prince of Peace" (Isaiah 9:6).
>
> "So Gideon built an altar there to the Lord, and called it The-Lord-Is-Peace" (Judges 6:24).
>
> "The peace of God, which surpasses all understanding" (Philippians 4:7).

The peace we're talking about comes from God. It finds its origin in God. Paul declared Him the God of peace. Isaiah prophesied He will be called the Prince of Peace.

Gideon discovered Him as Yahweh Shalom.

In Judges 6, Gideon found himself in a discouraged and fearful spot. His nation had done evil in the sight of the Lord and so God delivered them into the hand of their enemies. God raised Gideon up to deliver them from the hand of their enemies. Gideon, renowned for doubting himself and his qualification to serve God, had plenty of "prove it to me" moments with God.

It was in the first "test" that he discovered God as The-Lord-Is-Peace. Peace not only comes from God; it is actually part of His nature. This revelation came to a man who was hiding, discouraged, disappointed, doubting, and afraid. God came to him as Peace; Wholeness; Shalom.

God doesn't reveal Himself for Himself. He knows who He is. He does it for you. We're the ones who need to know who He is. Julie Winter said, "Through knowing Him, we are given the ability to participate in the very nature of God. God's nature is not one of depression, anxiety, or fear but of love, hope, peace, and joy. We have access to this nature by knowing Him."[10] The nature of God is revealed to show us what we get to participate in.

> Grace and peace be yours in abundance *through the knowledge of God and of Jesus our Lord.*
>
> His divine power has given us everything we need for a godly life through our knowledge of him who called us by his own glory and goodness.

> Through these he has given us his very great and precious promises, so that through them *you may participate in the divine nature*, having escaped the corruption in the world caused by evil desires.
>
> —2 Peter 1:2–4 NIV (emphasis mine)

In the inexhaustible nature of who God is, one way to describe Him is Peace: He is completely whole, lacking nothing, and overflowing. He is health, prosperity, tranquility, and contentment. He is unshakeable, immoveable, and unintimidated. He is fully secure in who He is.

Isn't this everything that everyone has ever wanted?

This is peace.

He is Peace.

A Prayer to Get You There

Lord Jesus, I recognize that peace comes from You and that You, Yourself, are Peace. Come with the substance of Your peace and fill my heart and mind. Show me any contrary voices that need to be replaced with Your truth and remind me of who I am in Christ. I yield myself to You.

— 3 —

THE GOSPEL OF PEACE

He was pierced for our transgressions,
he was crushed for our iniquities;
the punishment that brought us peace was on him,
and by his wounds we are healed.
—Isaiah 53:5 NIV

Almost twenty years ago now, I had one of the most impactful moments with God that I've ever had. Even though I had Christian overtones in my upbringing, I never really understood the cross. I received Jesus at seventeen years old because He made Himself real to me, but I still didn't understand what Jesus did for me at the cross.

Until one day, I was reading my Bible after church. I came across that powerful verse in Isaiah 53:5; specifically, the line that said, "The punishment that brought us peace was on him," and in an instant, God opened my eyes.

I finally saw that Jesus took my place at the cross. The punishment that brought me peace was *on Him.* I was overwhelmed by His mercy and full of gratitude.

My worship went to a whole new level as well as my entire relationship with God.

Looking at it now, I see even more. At the heart of the gospel is God's desire that we'd live in peace. In fact, the gospel is actually called the gospel of peace! And it's promised to be a message of peace.

> "Having shod your feet with the preparation of *the gospel of peace*" (Ephesians 6:15).
>
> "Behold, on the mountains
> The feet of him who brings good tidings,
> Who proclaims *peace*!" (Nahum 1:15).
>
> "How beautiful upon the mountains
> Are the feet of him who brings good news,
> Who proclaims *peace*" (Isaiah 52:7).
>
> "How welcome is the arrival of those proclaiming *the joyful news of peace* and of good things to come!" (Romans 10:15 TPT).

Peace Was Purchased

As we've looked at already, Jesus endured the punishment that brought us peace and wholeness. To reiterate one more time, shalom means: peace, completeness, soundness, welfare, health, prosperity, tranquility, and contentment; it's nothing missing, nothing broken.

Looking even further, there's a Greek word that describes what Jesus bought for us with His life. Its definition is encompassed in the word peace. It's the word *soteria.* It's where we get our English word *salvation.* You'll find it in verses like this: "For I am not ashamed of the gospel of Christ, for it is the power of God to *salvation* for everyone who believes, for the Jew first and also for the Greek." (Romans 1:16).

Apostle Paul is telling us that he's not ashamed of the gospel because it is the explosive, dynamic, supernatural ability of God to get people into a realm called "salvation" or *soteria*. The gospel is the powerful avenue through which people get there.

What, then, is *soteria*?

Soteria is being set free from the harassment of your enemies. It means rescue, preservation, safety, deliverance, salvation, health.[11] It's rooted in another Greek word, *sozo*, which means to save, keep safe and sound, to rescue from danger or destruction, to make well, heal, restore to health.[12]

This salvation was meant to elevate the quality of our entire lives. It was meant to impact our spirit, soul, and body. In the area of peace, it means being set free from the harassment of enemies like fear, anxiety, stress, shame, and insecurity. Jesus paid for us to be delivered from mental health issues and be completely healed and whole in our bodies.

Accepting Jesus sure does give us a home in heaven, but it should also elevate the quality of our lives in the here and now. It was meant to change the way we view life and the world around us; to see through the lens of the God who sits in heaven and laughs at His enemies. God's intention is to restore us to His image.

Peace and Harmony

> It pleased the Father that in Him all the fullness should dwell, and by Him to reconcile all things to Himself, by Him, whether things on earth or things in heaven, having made peace through the blood of His cross.
>
> —Colossians 1:19–20

The words for "reconcile" and "made peace" in Greek help us to see what exactly happened when Jesus' blood was shed.

> *Reconcile*—to reconcile completely, to reconcile back again, bring back to a former state of harmony.[13]
>
> *Made peace*—to make peace, establish harmony.[14]

Harmony simply means agreement. It's what happens in music when multiple notes combine to make a pleasing sound. Harmony puts color to music. It brings a sense of fullness, richness, and vibrancy.

We've all heard what it sounds like when that doesn't happen.... I call that the "bless your heart" ministry. We used to have a lady who would always come to the front of church during praise and worship and sing an octave higher than everyone in the room...and slightly flat. It was so piercing that, needless to say, people were distracted. I mean, bless her heart, she loved Jesus...but that joyful noise was tough to endure.

When musical notes are off, or not harmonizing, it's called dissonance. I would describe dissonance as unpleasant, discord, harsh sounding, state of unrest, needing completion, unresolved, or disagreement.

When I was taking music in college, we had to do an exercise in what's called atonality. Atonality is defined as the absence of key or tonal center.[15] In other words, there's no standard or base note to go by; it's a free for all. It's basically putting a bunch of notes together that don't work together...and it sounds horrible; like, imagine a cat screeching in labor while running its nails down a chalkboard. It's what they use in horror movies, so that what you hear matches the horror of what you see, creating a *horrible* experience.

That kind of dissonance creates an agitated, unsettled, stressful, and anxious sound. It paints a perfect picture of what sin and darkness does in a person's life. Jesus came to put everything back in order—in peace and harmony.

Back in Order

Just like atonality is defined as the absence of a tonal center, our lives were without the ultimate standard of God's Word. Sin knocked us off-course. Jesus' blood was shed to remove the dissonance from our lives and put us back in harmony or agreement. Agreement with what? With God's original design. He took the dissonant horror song and gave us a vibrant new song! (see Ps. 40:3).

Peace put us back in harmony. Harmony, then, means to be put back in order. Look at how these modern translations put Colossians 1:20—

> "By the blood of his cross, everything in heaven and earth is brought back to himself—*back to its original intent, restored to innocence again*!" (TPT).

> "All the broken and dislocated pieces of the universe—people and things, animals and atoms—get properly fixed and fit together in vibrant harmonies, all because of his death, his blood that poured down from the cross" (MSG).

When each note is in its proper place, the orchestra sounds amazing. Look at that again: "All the broken and dislocated pieces...get properly fixed and fit together in vibrant harmonies"! Peace puts things back in order.

We had been so off-course our whole lives that God sent Jesus to restore us spirit, soul, and body. Since this salvation affects the whole of our being, God wants to re-align us entirely.

Our spirit is born again when we receive Jesus. We were dead in sin but made alive in Christ. We've passed from death to life and are now co-heirs with Christ. We are God's "workmanship, created in Christ Jesus for good works, which God prepared beforehand that we should walk in them" (Eph. 2:10).

Bodies are healed by the finished work of the cross. The mere fact that our bodies have immune systems tells us that God created us to be healthy and to fight off disease. Disease was never meant to be welcome in our bodies. This is why Jesus went around teaching, preaching, and healing all who were sick proclaiming the kingdom of God. He was setting things back in order—and demonstrating it visually by healing people of *all kinds* of sickness and disease.

Last year, I was ministering on a livestream service for a fiery church in the Bay Area of California. God highlighted a young girl to me on the Zoom call and I saw her playing volleyball and asked if she did that. She told me she played sports but could no longer play because of a blood condition called iron deficiency anemia, which causes lethargy.

I realized I was in a God-ordained moment since just a week before that I was talking with some friends about another young man who was healed of anemia! I briefly shared the testimony and prayed for her healing; her mother prayed as well.

She later testified and said, "After that, believing that I was already healthy, I took a step of faith and stopped taking my iron pills. When I told the doctor that I was no longer taking my pills at my appointment last Saturday, she gave me a worried look like I was a little crazy. A few minutes later the nurse came into the room and told us that my iron levels were normal!" Praise God!

What was that? That was God putting things back in order in her body. I love how Isaiah 40:4 says that "the crooked places shall be made straight." He'll take all kinds of sickness, disease, pain, and ailments out of people's bodies and set them in heaven's order. Sickness is crookedness and it needs to be eradicated. This is what peace comes to do.

Renovated on the Inside

Finally, our souls—our mind, will, and emotions—become renovated through the Holy Spirit and the gospel of peace.

Like a tuning fork provides a sure standard for tuning a piano, the truth of God's Word found in scripture gives the ultimate standard to tune our lives to.

In the beginning, the earth was formless and void and there was darkness. You could say it was a place of chaos, emptiness, and confusion. But the Spirit of God was hovering over the waters (see Gen. 1:1–2). The Hebrew word for "hovering" can mean to be moved with the feeling of tender love, or to cherish.[16] Then God spoke and the chaos came into order.

Later on, apostle Paul would say the same narrative of creation happened again at salvation (see 2 Cor. 4:6). God, in His love, speaks over the chaos of our lives and brings order. It's the Word of God through the Agent of the Holy Spirit that puts us in God's original design. It's not just at salvation; He still hovers and still speaks over every area in our lives that needs His order.

You may have heard the phrase from the old KJV Bible, "For as he thinketh in his heart, so is he" (Proverbs 23:7). It's not that everything you think about yourself is true, it's that it's true *for you.* Craig Groeschel said it like this: "Our lives are always moving in the direction of our strongest thoughts…a lie believed as truth will affect your life as if it were true."[17]

Our world has bought into the lie that our thoughts define our identity. Just because you *think* it, doesn't mean you *are* it! The reality is, we all have "out of order" thoughts at times. It's when "out of order" thoughts begin to define us that the dissonance is perpetuated in our lives. But God's Word received in our lives sets everything in order; it puts everything in its proper place. We need His Word. This is what Jesus had in mind when He shed His blood.

Harmony. Order. Peace.

Blessed Are The Peacemakers

> "Blessed are the peacemakers, for they shall be called sons of God" (Matthew 5:9).

This gives us a whole new perspective on this powerful one-liner from the Sermon on the Mount. Peacemakers aren't passive people-pleasers, they're people who put things back in order! They *make* peace. They put things in their proper place. Peacemaking is like setting a broken bone. Where people or things are out of God's will, peacemakers work to set it right.

Essentially, this is the ministry of Jesus. Where people were harassed by demons, Jesus brought the kingdom and cast them out. Where people were weighed down by sickness and disease, Jesus set their bodies back in order and healed them. Where people were burdened by rigid religion, Jesus showed them what a real relationship with the Father looked like. Where people were confused about who God was and who they were, He spoke His life-giving Word and began to put things in order.

Everywhere Jesus went, He set things in order. Where Adam marred the image of how we were meant to live, Jesus came as the perfect prototype, demonstrating our purpose. When we do the peacemaking work of the kingdom, we will be called sons of God. Why? Because we look just like Jesus, *the* Son of God.

Peacemaking isn't stirring up problems but putting things in order. Conflict may be necessary, but the goal isn't more chaos, it's order. When Jesus spoke to the storm and calmed it, He demonstrated what it's like to put things in their proper place.

Shalom Is Victorious

One night, a while back, a group of friends and I went to a local Denny's after church. I was introduced to a Messianic rabbi who was there studying. He shared with us a powerful revelation on the Hebrew word for peace: *shalom*.

SHALOM/PEACE

(Ancient Hebrew)

SHIN:
Picture of teeth; it can mean to **destroy** because you crush food with them.

LAMED:
Picture of shepherd's staff; it symbolizes **authority**.

VAV:
Picture of a nail; it can mean **attach** because you use a nail to connect one thing to another.

MEM:
Picture of waters; in this context, it can mean **chaos** (as in the flood).

Putting these pictograph meanings together you get:

"Destroy (the) authority (that) attaches (to) chaos"

Each letter of the Hebrew alphabet has multiple dimensions of meaning. It has the regular phonic meaning, a numerical value, as well as a pictograph meaning. The pictograph meaning comes from the Ancient Hebrew letters. I believe there's a prophetic message hidden within the pictograph meaning of the word *shalom*, which you can see in the image on the previous page. (NOTE: Hebrew reads from right to left.)

It's like the author of shalom is telling us: peace comes when the authority that attaches to chaos is destroyed. Hidden within the word *shalom* is the victory that Jesus won at the cross. *Jesus destroyed the authority that attaches you to chaos and made the way for you to have peace. Receive His victory and peace!*

Look at how Colossians 2:13–15 TPT explains this:

> This "realm of death" describes our former state, for we were held in sin's grasp. But now, we've been resurrected out of that "realm of death" never to return, for we are forever alive and forgiven of all our sins!
>
> He canceled out every legal violation we had on our record and the old arrest warrant that stood to indict us. He erased it all—our sins, our stained soul—he deleted it all and they cannot be retrieved! Everything we once were in Adam has been placed onto his cross and nailed permanently there as a public display of cancellation.
>
> Then Jesus made a public spectacle of all the powers and principalities of darkness, stripping away from them every weapon and all their spiritual authority and power to accuse us.

> And by the power of the cross, Jesus led them around as prisoners in a procession of triumph. He was not their prisoner; they were his!

Wow! And these scriptures as well:

> "Since the children have flesh and blood, he too shared in their humanity so that by his death he might *break the power* of him who holds the power of death—that is, the devil—and free those who all their lives were held in slavery by their fear of death" (Hebrews 2:14–15 NIV emphasis mine).
>
> Jesus came and spoke to them, saying, "*All authority* has been given to Me in heaven and on earth" (Matthew 28:18, emphasis mine).

Jesus defeated the authority of our sin and the devil at the cross. Everything that attached us to chaos – our sins, guilt, shame, fear, condemnation, the lies and works of the enemy, and the enemy himself – has been defeated at the cross. There's forgiveness and freedom from chaos in Christ!

Every time Jesus showed His scars after the resurrection, He spoke peace to His disciples. Being that Jesus was Jewish, He used the word *shalom*. Now you know that He was also declaring the victory that frees you from chaos. Receive it and enforce it in your life today.

Let's add all of this to our definition of peace: God's order, vibrant harmony, and *freedom from chaos*.

The Goal of the Gospel

Ultimately, Jesus died so we could have peace with God. There's nothing like knowing that you've been forgiven and accepted completely by God. If you haven't taken that step yet, call on the Lord Jesus. Accept Him as Your Lord and Savior and turn from sin. (For more, see Appendix 2).

The goal of the gospel is peace; putting everything back in order. Jesus paid to rid your life of dissonance and chaos and put you back into vibrant harmony. No wonder the angel announced that the coming of Jesus was good news of great joy for all people! Heaven burst forth in praise saying, "Glory to God in the highest, and on earth *peace*, goodwill toward men!" (Luke 2:11, 14).

A Prayer to Get You There

Lord Jesus, thank You for Your sacrifice on the cross. Thank You that all the dislocated and broken pieces of my life get put back together in vibrant harmonies because of what You've done for me. I receive Your forgiveness and freedom. I receive healing in my body and health in my soul. You paid to make me whole. Thank You that You free me from chaos. Let Your peace rule in my heart and mind.

Activation

Take communion and gratefully meditate on what Jesus accomplished for you on the cross.

— 4 —

FIERCER THAN THE STORM

You only have authority over
the storm you can sleep in.
—Bill Johnson

A while ago, I was flying back home from a mission trip to the Philippines. It's always exciting to see people come to Jesus and encounter His love. On the flight, we hit some kind of storm, and then came the turbulence. Heavy turbulence. I wish I could say I was God's man of power for the hour and commanded the storm to cease...but that wasn't the case. I was freaked out. I thought I was gonna die.

Meanwhile, my good friend was sitting next to me—in a deep sleep. As the turbulence lifted and dropped the plane, his head—mouth open—was bobbing to the beat of the bumpy ride...completely oblivious to the fact that we were all about to die! I can still see the scene replaying in my head.

I may be exaggerating a little bit—we're all alive today—but the fact remains that we were both on the same plane, going to the same place, except, while one of us was freaking out in fear, the other one was peacefully resting in a deep sleep. He was so deep in sleep that the turbulence didn't disturb him. Sound familiar?

Jesus and His disciples had a similar experience—except not in the air, stuck in a metal tube flying through a typhoon. They were on a boat in the middle of a life-threatening storm. Not sure which is worse. The good news is peace was found in both.

> That same day, after it grew dark, Jesus said to his disciples, "Let's cross over to the other side of the lake." Leaving the crowd behind, the disciples got into the boat in which Jesus was already sitting, and they took him with them. Other boats sailed with them. Suddenly, as they were crossing the lake, a ferocious storm arose, with violent winds and waves that were crashing into the boat until it was nearly swamped. But Jesus was calmly sleeping in the stern, resting on a cushion.
>
> —Mark 4:35–38 TPT

Sometimes the way we picture peace is looking out over a calm lake, reclining back during the sunset while the kids are getting along quite nicely. While I don't disagree with this image, I think it's more relevant to picture peace as what we see above: Jesus sleeping in a boat in the middle of a life-threatening storm. It's what we've been saying all along: Peace is an inner reality that is unshaken by outward circumstances. Jesus demonstrated what peace looks like and leads us by example.

Sleeping in the Storm

The one thing Jesus said to His disciples before they got in the boat was, "Let's cross over to the other side of the lake." He planned on getting to the other side. We could say it like this: They had a word from God that they were getting to the other side of the lake.

Then Jesus fell asleep. Why? To put it practically, He was tired. Charles Spurgeon said it like this: "Christ was weary and worn; and when anyone is exhausted, it is his duty to go to sleep if he can. The Saviour must be up again in the morning, preaching and working miracles, and if He does not sleep, He will not be fit for His holy duty; it is incumbent upon Him to keep Himself in trim for His service."[18] We glorify God best when we're in rest.

To the point: Jesus slept because He trusted God. He slept in the stern on a pillow and left the helm to His Father. That's not apprehensively sleeping with one eye open hoping that the disciples will potentially steer the ship to safety. That's full on going into a deep sleep—finding a quiet place in the back of the boat, away from the steering wheel, relinquishing control to the Father, and grabbing a cushion to rest your head on. Jesus rested because He trusted His Father who was in charge of it all.

He knew His Father would get them to the other side. "We'll be fine…Abba is taking care of us…I'm tired, I'm going to sleep." He had full confidence in His Father—which is where rest comes from. He was able to sleep because He was in rest—not just a physical rest, but a rest in His soul. He was living from the higher reality of the Father's love and protection. *That's* rest. How do you sleep in the storm? Do what Jesus did.

When the circumstance changed (i.e., the storm), it didn't change His rest because the storm wasn't managing His peace—the Father was; and He *is* peace. On the inside, He was still resting by the still waters, while on the outside the storm raged on. The storm clouds may have covered the sky, but the sun was still shining above the clouds.

Rest is directly connected to who you believe is in charge and how you view them. I remember having the hardest time sleeping in the car on a road trip I did with some friends in my late teens. I really didn't trust the other dudes driving! When they had the steering wheel, technically they were in charge, but the problem was they were young, immature, driving 100 mph, and one of the guys just didn't seem to care much. It just felt a bit reckless. My rest was definitely spotty, and I opted to drive most of the time. But Jesus trusted God and knew He was in charge—and knew He was good and trustworthy. Therefore, He could fully rest. We would do well to follow His example.

I was meditating in prayer one day on the sea of glass like crystal found before the throne of God (Rev. 4:6). To me, it's reminiscent of the still waters that David rested by in Psalm 23:2. It represents peace. What struck me, though, was that there is lightning and thundering proceeding out of the throne. I'd imagine that any type of sea would be shaken up with that kind of power and rumbling so close to it!

God said that He would shake everything that can be shaken (Heb. 12:27–28). Yet that's exactly it—His peace *cannot* be shaken. It's a prophetic parable illustrating the unshakeable nature of His peace. We know the rumbling from the throne is good. It's coming from *His* throne! But in regard to any type of shaking going on in our lives, His peace remains unshakeable.

This is a peace that is stronger than the storm. This is what Jesus slept in. Rest was His defense against the storm—and it can be yours too.

Manage Your Heart

Note that it wasn't the storm that shook Jesus awake, it was His disciples. "So they shook him awake, saying, 'Teacher, don't you even care that we are all about to die!'" (Mark 4:39 TPT).

The storm around them became the storm inside them. And whenever the storm around you becomes the storm within you, it distorts your perception of reality. It affected how they saw God—they accused Jesus of not caring. It affected how they saw themselves—they believed they were going to die. It affected how they saw their circumstances—they saw it as the end. If you were there, you may have heard them say, "We're dying over here and You're sleeping?!"

To reiterate what was said in Chapter 2, whoever holds the narrative in your life holds your perception of reality. And out of that—your functionality, and ultimately your destiny. The disciples let the storm hold the narrative. Don't let the storm hold the narrative!

We need to calm the storm inside of us so we can handle the storms around us. Proverbs 18:14 says it like this: "The human spirit can endure in sickness, but a crushed spirit who can bear?" (NIV). In other words, it's what's going on in the inside that matters. If you can manage your inner world, you can handle what goes on in the "outer" world.

Today, we've been bombarded by all kinds of "storms" trying to hinder the word and work of God in our lives. From politics, raging injustice, news media outlets to health issues, mental health issues, relational and financial issues. Then there are the inner storms of a lack of value for ourselves, condemnation, shame, and fear. For example, if you don't believe in yourself and what God says about you, then it doesn't matter what life throws at you; you will always feel inadequate to handle it.

We need the greater narrative of God's Word to uphold us.

Years ago, a prominent healing minister came to my city to do a healing and impartation conference. Surprise, surprise—not everyone enjoys the full gospel of Jesus; the Jesus who supernaturally saves, heals, and delivers. So, some demonstrators came and protested outside of the church where the conference was being held.

On our way in, I caught wind of what one of the protesters was saying. I didn't agree and decided I'd speak my mind. Not the best choice. We got into a bit of an argument, and I felt like a guard dog when an intruder comes around. You know, when the hair on their spine stands up and they're walking on edge. My adrenaline was pumping.

I realized I let his critical and argumentative spirit stir up the still waters in me and cause a storm of fleshly anger. I should've slept on that storm and moved right along. Instead, I let his storm make a storm in me.

Jesus said this: "Peace I leave with you; my peace I give you. I do not give to you as the world gives. Do not let your hearts be troubled and do not be afraid" (John 14:27 NIV). Sleep on the storms and rest in the Lord. Don't let the storms around you become the storms inside you.

Follow the Leader

Years ago, I took a bunch of youth and young adults to a super charismatic conference. We were hungry for more of God and His supernatural power to move. But we were relatively new to what we were about to encounter.

At the end of the service, we experienced our first "fire tunnel." If you're not familiar with that, it's a creative way to pray for people. You make a "tunnel" by having two lines of people standing opposite and facing each other. Then you send people down the tunnel and the people that formed the tunnel pray for them. It can get pretty wild...in a good way.

Being that our group was new to this stuff, there were three types of groups within our one group. The first group was ALL IN. They were ready for more and got blasted by the power of God and filled with His joy. The second group was standing off to the side, apprehensive about the activity. The third group was standing way off with their arms folded angrily. They thought it was irreverent to treat the Holy Spirit that way.

People were laughing hysterically under the joy of the Lord, rolling on the ground and falling down. Some people got so filled with God that we had to carry two of the girls in our group to the vehicles because they couldn't walk anymore.

The kicker for the second and third groups was that one of our senior pastors was also with us on this trip. She jumped right in and received a mighty touch of God's power and joy. The logic went like this: If one of our spiritual moms is going in, then we feel safe to follow her lead!

We decided to take our cues from our leader and not our fear. There was a trust that was developed and many followed her right in...and had a blast. If she could do it, then we could too! Let me just say it again: *We trusted our leader and not our fear.*

Why did the disciples freak out? *They let the storm lead them and not Jesus.*

The text doesn't tell us every detail of the story, but I wonder if any of the disciples considered taking their cues from Jesus instead of the storm. Did anybody stop to wonder *why* or *how* Jesus was sleeping in this storm? They might've thought, "If He is that restful, either He's crazy, maybe just extremely exhausted...or *I am missing out on something that He's got.* I need whatever He has." We know that He had an anchor locked into His Father's love.

Furthermore, did anyone consider following Jesus' example? "He's not freaking out, so I don't have to, either. If He can sleep, then so can I!" They could've taken their cues from His restfulness and approach the storm from that place instead of from raging anxiety.

Anxiety clouds your viewpoint, but rest and peace give clarity on reality.

I think one of the greatest reasons why fear and anxiety run rampant in believers is because they let the storm lead them and not Jesus.

Say this out loud:

> The storm is not my leader.
>
> Jesus is.
>
> Fear is not my leader.
>
> Jesus is.
>
> _______________ is not my leader.
>
> Jesus is.
>
> I take my cues from Him.

The Storm Has a Voice

"Then He arose and rebuked the wind, and said to the sea, 'Peace, be still!' And the wind ceased and there was a great calm" (Mark 4:39). The Greek word for "peace" in this verse isn't the same one we've been studying, but it does serve to expand our definition of the nature of peace. It's actually a command that means to be silent and is rooted in a word that means involuntary stillness or inability to speak.[19] In other words, forced into silence.

The word for "be still" is similar and means to close the mouth with a muzzle, to stop the mouth, to make speechless, reduce to silence, to be kept in check.[20]

The fact that Jesus told the storm to be involuntarily quiet and muzzled tells us that the storm had a voice. Jesus shut the mouth of this storm. Peace doesn't allow contrary voices to have a voice in its atmosphere.

One time, after a church service, a lady came up to my friend and started giving this shame-filled, manipulative prophetic (I should say pathetic) word. I confronted her and essentially told her we don't do that here and she didn't have the authority to minister. She didn't listen, and after multiple attempts to stop her from speaking, something rose up within me and I told her to shut her mouth. I realize I was most likely speaking to a spirit. She still didn't listen. Long story short, she got kicked out and has never returned. This is not a frequent habit of mine, but it ended up being a running joke I like to call the "shut your mouth ministries."

It's shutting down the mouth of the storm. While I don't make it a common practice to shut people down, I consistently shut down the contrary voices that try to speak internally. You have the authority to silence those voices.

On that boat, Jesus exemplified to us how to deal with contrary voices—shut them up. Don't allow them to have a voice in your life. Treat them like you do the telemarketers who are always trying to get at you on the phone—hit the red button and DECLINE (no offense if you're a telemarketer).

The Power of Hearing

As I've been reading the context of Mark 4, I realize that the entire chapter leading up to this story is about hearing. Jesus told the Parable of the Sower, which is all about the ability to receive the Word (which starts with hearing). He said twice to them, "If anyone has ears to hear, let him hear," and the word for "hear" was mentioned fourteen times in this one chapter.

Mark 4:33 says, "And with many such parables He spoke the word to them as they were *able to hear it*" (emphasis mine).

Then in Mark 4:35, we see this: "*On the same day*, when evening had come, *He said to them*, 'Let us cross over to the other side'" (emphasis mine).

On the same day as He was teaching them about the power of hearing, He speaks again to them *in their hearing* and says, "Let us cross over to the other side." But then another voice comes in direct opposition to what Jesus just told them.

There are three voices here: the voice of Jesus, the voice of the storm, and the voice of the disciples. The disciples heard both the voice of Jesus and the voice of the storm. Instead of aligning with the voice of Jesus, the disciples bought into the voice of the storm, and their voice began to vocalize what the storm was telling them:

> "Teacher, do You not care that we are perishing?" (Mark 4:38).
>
> "Lord, save us! We are perishing!" (Matthew 8:25).
>
> "Master, Master, we are perishing!" (Luke 8:24).

The storm told them they were going to die, and they let the storm hold the narrative. It was like the disciples internalized the storm's threats, and it came out of their mouths. No one seemed to remember what Jesus told them. Jesus said they'd get to the other side; they said they were dying.

Our English word "worry" is rooted in a word which means "to strangle."[21] In Mark 4:19, Jesus said it's the worries of this world that choke out the word. Worry got the best of them, and it choked out their faith and the word that Jesus spoke to them.

While Jesus shut the mouth of the storm, the disciples disregarded the voice of Jesus. The disciples *let* the storm have a voice in their life, and it ended up taking a higher place in their hearts than what Jesus told them. What if the lack of peace that people experience isn't because of the presence of a storm, it's because we haven't listened to the right voice?

What's encouraging about this story is that we get to see what went wrong and learn from it. Instead of disregarding the voice of Jesus in our lives, we can lock into His voice, follow Jesus' example, and shut the mouth of the storm! Refuse to let the storm have a voice in your life.

THE VOICE OF DOUBT

James 1:6 says, "But let him ask in faith, with no doubting, for he who doubts is like a wave of the sea driven and tossed by the wind."

> No stability.
> No firm foundation.
> No anchor point.
> Just pushed around.
> Being moved by the wind of every storm.

The storm they went through was the exact same thing—waves driven and tossed by the wind. Mark 4:37 says, "A great windstorm arose, and the waves beat into the boat." It was a visual manifestation of doubt. In fact, the original word for "wave" means a violent agitation of the sea, and it's only used here in James 1:6 and in Luke's account of the story (Luke 8:24). The storm's voice was the voice of doubt.

By listening to the voice of doubt, it caused the disciples to doubt Jesus' word about them getting to the other side. They internalized the voice of doubt, and it came overflowing out of their mouths. They were driven and tossed by the wind, not calmed and confident by the Word.

They took on the nature of the voice they believed in.

Selah.

If we're honest, we've taken on the wrong nature at times—fearful, anxious, shaken—because we've listened to the wrong voice. But it also works conversely. We can take on the nature of Jesus by faith—calm, confident, restful, authoritative—and have a fierce peace that weathers the storms.

Whose Voice Will You Believe?

Earlier that day, when Jesus explained the Parable of the Sower, He told the disciples: "Others, like seed sown on rocky places, hear the word and at once receive it with joy. But since they have no root, they last only a short time. *When trouble or persecution comes because of the word, they quickly fall away*" (Mark 4:16–17 NIV, emphasis mine).

Wait a second... Trouble or persecution comes *because* of the word? That's what Jesus said.

I remember years ago, when I was pastoring my church's young adult group, one of our students came up with a question. She said the verse that God had been speaking to her was 2 Corinthians 5:17— "Therefore, if anyone is in Christ, he is a new creation; old things have passed away; behold, all things have become new." She said the problem was that all of these people from her past kept showing up in her life in random ways. She was a bit confused and wondered if she should be ministering to them. With young adults, usually when your past comes calling, it's a good idea to walk the other way.

That's called persecution because of the word! God was establishing the truth in her heart, and it was attracting persecution. The enemy wanted to tempt her to fall away from that truth and return to her past; but God was using those circumstances to further establish truth in her heart. She had the opportunity to fully embrace her new life in Christ while in the face of her past.

For the disciples on the boat, they dealt with persecution and trouble as the storm came and confronted them with the opposite of what Jesus said to them. The fallacy that many believers fall into is that if God gives us a word, then the circumstances will automatically line up with it. That can happen, but it's not always the case. Sometimes your circumstances will look completely opposite to what God has said. You've got to stand on the word regardless of what you see.

The fork in the road comes to give us a choice on what word we're going to believe.

What has the storm been telling you?

What has God been speaking to you?

Whose voice will you believe?

Faith Training

"He said to them, 'Why are you so fearful? How is it that you have no faith?'" (Mark 4:40). Take a second and remember who Jesus is talking to. These are the main guys we look up to as the fathers of our faith. Some of them wrote the scriptures we read and became the foundations of the church. All that to say: If you've ever battled fear and struggled with faith, you're in good company! Don't let shame get on you during your journey of faith. God is still for you.

Jesus asked them some pointed questions. I don't know about you, but I imagine Jesus asking those questions with a bit of frustration and disappointment as if He was speaking with the same sternness as He did to the storm. But what if He was genuinely asking them with a compassionate fatherly tone? What if the whole story was a setup to develop the disciples' faith? I don't think it was a chiding remark; rather, it was a moment in faith training.

Jesus isn't asking questions to get information. He's doing it so that we can get revelation about our condition, and from there, position ourselves for breakthrough.

"How did you get to this place? Could you possibly have the rocky or thorny soil that didn't properly nourish the seed of the word that I spoke?"

"Did you let the storm command you? What got you to a lack of peace?"

Jesus said they were filled with fear and had no faith. It's the same thing going on in our world today. Anxiety and fear are draining our faith and peace. The disciples were intimidated! Intimidation welcomes in whatever you're intimidated by and kills faith. Faith tests allow you to see what you really believe. When your faith is challenged, it allows an opportunity for faith to become strengthened.

I believe that Jesus can and will calm the storms in our lives. But Jesus' response to the disciples in the boat tells me He was training them for more than that. It's one thing to have Jesus calm the storms for us; it's another thing to learn how to silence the mouth of the storms ourselves. He was training them to walk in faith and authority.

Specifically, Jesus asked them about their faith. Your beliefs either keep you under the circumstance or lift you over the circumstance. Your beliefs are formed by what you listen to. What you give heed to is what forms your perception and approach to every circumstance. I know I've come at this from multiple angles, but here's the question: What are you consistently hearing? In other words, who's dominating in your environment? When the storm around you starts raging within you, you lose your authority to speak to the storm. Yet there's a way to rise above. You can silence the storms when you're living above them.

HOW DAVID DID IT

David was able to defeat Goliath because he wasn't listening to the giant talk trash for forty days. All of

Israel was dismayed and terrified because of what they were listening to (i.e., the giant's trash talking). David came from the shepherd fields where he was found as a man after God's own heart. His atmosphere was no doubt filled with a consciousness of the nature and Presence of God. He came from a higher reality.

When he came on the scene and heard Goliath's trash talk, it was appalling and completely foreign to him. It was unnatural for him to tolerate that type of talk. It was a voice that needed to be dealt with. It's like David said, "Where I come from, this is not allowed!"

In other words, he wasn't under the influence of the giant's taunting, he was under the influence of God's dominion. He was lifted higher than his enemies. He said it like this:

> One thing I have desired of the Lord,
> That will I seek:
> That I may dwell in the house of the Lord
> All the days of my life,
> To behold the beauty of the Lord...
> For in the time of trouble
> He shall hide me in His pavilion;
> In the secret place of His tabernacle
> He shall hide me;
> He shall set me high upon a rock.
> *And now my head shall be lifted up above my enemies all around me.*
>
> —Psalm 27:4–6 (emphasis mine)

His devotion to the Lord caused him to be lifted up higher than his enemies. That's not just reading a book, that's entering an atmosphere. The atmosphere of God's presence. That atmosphere affects the way you think, see, and feel. It affects all your perceptions.

I believe there's a realm of faith that is accessible to us that doesn't hear those contrary voices; and if they are heard, they have no power to affect the hearer. David said, "My head shall be lifted up *above* my enemies."

So, what did David do? He cut off the giant's head—the thing that had been yapping all that time. He took the giant out and literally silenced him. He refused to let the giant have a voice in his life and the life of his people. Position your heart like David did— meditating on His Word, spending time in worship and prayer, beholding God. This is what cultivates good soil that produces a faith filled harvest.

Jesus, the Son of David, without a doubt lived in that reality, in that atmosphere of God's presence. He lived in a heightened consciousness and awareness of God.

DRAW FROM JESUS

Instead of letting the storm around you become the storm within you, let the Lord around you become the Lord within you. The disciples had two atmospheres around them: the raging storm and the resting Lord. It's important to deny the voice of the storm that's raging, but it's even more important to draw from the Lord that's resting.

The disciples obviously drew from the raging storm, but what would've happened if they drew from Jesus? Yes, it's important to block the storms from getting in, but also let Peace come in! Welcome peace, welcome faith, welcome joy, welcome rest, welcome love, welcome hope. Expect good things to come your way. The same way you've let the storm in, let the Lord in. Your weary soul needs the Presence of God.

Later in his life, David had a time when the circumstances were extremely distressing. An enemy raid had come through while they were gone, burning their city with fire and taking captive their wives, sons, and daughters. He and his men wept so much that they had no more power to weep. His own men were talking about stoning him, but the scripture said "David *drew strength* from the Lord his God." (1 Samuel 30:6 NET, emphasis mine). He went and took refuge in the Lord and drew life and strength from His Presence. From that place, he inquired of the Lord, pursued the enemy, overtook them, and recovered all.

David and his men were sapped of all their strength because the trial was so hard on them. Maybe you've felt the same way. You know you need to fight, but it's like trying to make withdrawals on a bank account that's in the negative, putting a demand on something that's not there. We have the same answer as David.

Draw strength from the Presence of the Lord. Draw from Jesus. Take refuge in Him. Jesus said that He is the Vine and we are the branches (John 15:5). The branches draw life from the vine. It's their life source. In every circumstance, we have the opportunity to take a moment to draw from the Lord who rests in the storm; to behold the One who is above it all; to let His rest and peace flood our hearts. From there, we'd be positioned to handle the storm with confidence and authority. We'd move from defense to *offense*.

"They were filled with great fear and said to one another, "Who then is this, that even the wind and the sea obey him?" (Mark 4:41). Jesus was definitely on the offense. His authority dominates over storms, spirits submit to Him, sickness listens to Him, and the atmosphere comes under attention to His Presence and command. In calming the storm, He was displaying to the disciples what authority looked like—because they'd eventually take over and need to learn faith and authority. Authority flows out of rest. Rest is when you know who you are and you've settled it inside. He came from a place of rest and commanded the storm to cease.

Jesus took what was inside of Him and made it manifest outside of Him. Charles Spurgeon said, "We cannot create a calm till we are in a calm."[22] He was already living in rest so when He took authority over the storm, He put His atmosphere on the storm. It's like He said, "What's *in me*, be *in you*!" In fact, the word for "rest" in Greek means a *calming of the winds.*[23] His sleep on the boat in the middle of a life-threatening storm was a visual of what was living in Him all along—unshakeable peace. Whether He was asleep or awake, the rest remained.

This is the rest we're called to enter into—"Let us therefore be diligent to enter that rest." (Heb. 4:11). This is why we pull on Jesus. We draw from His rest, His faith, His strength, and His authority. As we receive from Him, we enter into that place of faith and rest where we live above the storms. Take a moment to turn your heart toward Jesus in gratitude and affection and watch as His Presence comes flooding in. Intimacy with God positions you for authority.

Is Jesus Sleeping in Your Boat?

Have you ever felt abandoned in your toughest trial? Like God wasn't present and helping you? I'm sure that's exactly what the disciples felt when Jesus was sleeping while they were frightened for their lives. "We're fighting for our lives over here and You're sleeping?! Don't You care? Hello? Are You there?" But here is what you need to know: If Jesus is sleeping in your storm, it's not a sign that He doesn't care about you; it's that He's not concerned with the storm. Remember, it wasn't the storm what woke Him up, it was the cries of His disciples. That should tell you what He really cares about.

It's important to see that He wasn't letting the storm get to Him. He's above it. And *He's inviting you to do the same.* He's leading by example. In fact, His first words to some of them were "Follow Me."

He's not concerned with the storm; He's concerned with you. But not in a coddling kind of way. You're not a victim to the storm; you're a student of the Lord. You can't see the storms as a victim. They're not the big bad guy coming to ruin your life. They are an opportunity to exercise your faith muscle. They are in your path so you can take dominion over them with the greater reality of the kingdom of God.

I remember having a piano teacher years ago who would always push me to grow. He would walk by and drop sheet music on my stand that, to me, felt way too advanced to learn for where I was at. But he saw something in me that made him believe I could handle it. It was his way of stretching me and calling me higher.

This is what happens when we go through trials. God sees our potential and is bringing us to a higher place of faith and trust in Him.

The scripture alludes to our faith being like gold refined in the fire (1 Peter 1:6–7). The fire brings the impurities to the surface so they can be removed, and the gold becomes purer. The fire of trials works to bring the unnecessary and unhealthy things in our lives to the surface so they can be removed. The result is a stronger, purer, and valuable faith—anchored in Jesus.

This is not to be insensitive to the tragedies and traumas people have faced. There's no shame if you're dealing with anxiety. It's just time to not let those things define you any longer. The devil wants to use the storms to take you out, but God wants to use them as training for reigning.

If you approach storms as a victim, you're already defeated. If you approach storms as a king, you overcome. In our house, when we face a difficult situation, we say, "There's always a way." In other words, instead of feeling stuck in any situation, we just believe there's always a way out. When you don't think there's a way out, you won't go looking for it. But if you believe there's always a way out, you'll find a way. If Jesus could make a way for us and rise up from the dead, surely there's a way to peace in any situation!

You get something by persevering that you don't get any other way. You get a tempered strength, a fortified vigor, and a staying power. Victims don't have that. Champions do—and that's what you are. You're not a victim; you're an overcomer.

Pages later, the same disciples that were fearful in the midst of the storm are in Book of Acts and they're standing up against the toughest persecution. In the storm, they were afraid of death, but in Acts, they had *no fear of death!*

What was happening in the storm? God was exposing the disciples to death so they could get over their fear of it. Psalm 23:3 says, "He leads me in the paths of righteousness for His name's sake." Then in the very next verse David says, "Yea, though I walk through the valley of the shadow of death, I will fear no evil; For You are with me." *The paths of righteousness include the valley of the shadow of death!* Why? So we'd learn to fear no evil! It's part of God's righteousness.

They were inoculated by a constant exposure to death. It's like the purest kind of vaccine (too soon?). God knew they'd need to have no fear of death in order to bear up under the weight of their future; so He exposed them to death multiple times. Not enough to take them out – but enough to build "immunity" against it (not that they wouldn't die, but that death wouldn't intimidate them). Then when Pentecost came, a supernatural boldness got on the disciples because they were filled with the same Spirit that conquered death and raised Jesus from the dead!

Jesus set them up for success. Jesus was training them. The storm was training ground for their faith. The trials you face now are preparing you to stand firm in your future. There's training in your trial.

God is strengthening your feeble legs so you can stand in faith (see Hebrews 12:12, Isaiah 35:3–4). You're not meant to take your promised land with feeble legs!

Fear made you feeble, but faith makes you fierce!

Conclusion

Let's recap.

- Jesus' peace is unshakeable.
- Don't let the storms around you become the storms inside you.
- The storm is not your leader, Jesus is.
- Refuse to let the storm have a voice in your life.
- Shut down the contrary voices.
- Be anchored in Jesus' word.
- Your storm is faith training.
- Develop deep, consistent devotion to Jesus.

Jesus didn't have a storm on the inside, so He could handle the storm on the outside. Our God is unshaken, unintimidated, and unmoved. In fact, He sits in the heavens and laughs (Ps. 2:4). Jesus sets the ultimate example for us to follow.

By the way, they made it to the other side. "Then they came to the other side of the sea, to the country of the Gadarenes" (Mark 5:1).

A Prayer to Get You There

Father, thanks that You gave us the ultimate example in Jesus. I yield myself to You and the Lordship of Jesus. Teach me Your ways. I open my heart to You, Lord, and draw strength from Your Presence. Thank You for faith and authority to shut down the contrary voices and speak to the storms. I will make it to the other side, in Jesus' name. Amen.

— 5 —

PEACE STANDS GUARD

Peace is not merely the absence of war but the presence of justice, of law, of order —in short, of government.

—Albert Einstein

In the introduction, I began to share about an encounter I had with the Prince of Peace. I was in a time of prayer, getting ready to preach that night when I felt like I walked into a wall of the Presence of God. I looked and saw in a vision a Man clothed in samurai armor. Not dressed in a robe and sandals, but in armor and with a sword. He held out His sword to me and touched my chest with it. I could physically feel the blade on me.

I realized that if this is the Lord, I shouldn't be standing, I should be on the ground. But since His sword was on me, I didn't go forward, I went backward until I was lying on my back on the ground. If I went on my face, that would mean something like humility, honor, or reverence. But I was on my back, which is a position of rest. Like how David said in Psalm 23:2, "He makes me to lie down."

His sword followed me down, and as I looked at the sword, it said "peace." He spoke to me and said very strongly, "Don't ever call My peace passive." He turned around and, with sword drawn, stood guard over me.

I knew I had encountered the Prince of Peace, and I knew that I had just experienced Philippians 4:6–7—

> Be anxious for nothing, but in everything by prayer and supplication, with thanksgiving, let your requests be made known to God; and the peace of God, which surpasses all understanding, will guard your hearts and minds through Christ Jesus.

In this chapter, I want to break down these verses to discover how we can activate this peace that guards.

FAITH FOCUSED

First off, Paul writes, "Be anxious for nothing." Seth Dahl says that Paul "is first and foremost telling us it is possible to not worry."[24] It's possible to not be anxious! Secondly, you're empowered to do it. And thirdly, we all face anxiety. He wouldn't be writing it if people didn't face it. In other words, again, we're in good company.

Anxiety wants to distract you. The Greek word for anxiety means to be drawn in different directions in your mind. The Passion Translation captures this well: "Don't be pulled in different directions or worried about a thing."

I remember one time at a church event hanging out with my wife and some friends at a table. Someone was there who I hadn't seen in a while, and I saw a quick vision for her and struck up a conversation. I asked, "Hey, have you been traveling lately?" She sarcastically retorted with a comment about her not being at church like I was about to rebuke her for it. Since I had been traveling for ministry, I had no idea of her church attendance.

Apparently, everyone at the table was shocked at her remark, wondering what I was going to say. The only thing was, I was oblivious to her slap back because I was caught up and focused on what I was about to prophesy. "Oh, interesting, because I see you traveling." Her defensive face dropped and she began to come out from the walls she seemed to be hiding behind.

That could've been a pretty "storm-filled" moment relationally for that table. But I was oblivious to her sarcasm. I was on another frequency. I wasn't fully present in the flesh; I was looking in the Spirit.

While anxiety wants to distract you, faith gives you focus. It's not just focus; it's faith. Faith puts you in the realm of the Spirit so you *can* focus. It's a different level of consciousness. It's seeing from Jesus' perspective and what the Father is doing. When anxiety is knocking on your door and trying to distract you, ask, "What is the Father doing? What is He saying?" Take that higher ground.

When we're under a flesh mindset, it's easy to be like the disciples who were freaking out on the boat while Jesus was sleeping during a life-threatening storm. If I'm left to the flesh, I'm left to reason. It's not logical or practical to sleep in the storm! But faith looks and lives on a deeper level. "Trust in the Lord with all your heart and lean not to your own understanding" (Prov. 3:5).

Faith puts you in the higher ways of God and heaven. (It's also not an excuse to be weird and irresponsible.)

If the storm can get you in the flesh, then it can dominate you. Jesus said, "It is the Spirit who gives life; the flesh profits nothing. The words that I speak to you are spirit, and they are life" (John 6:63).

I want to emphasize that this focus is not the world's way of doing things. If you type the word "focus" into your iPhone, the suggested emoji will be an image of someone meditating in an eastern cross-legged pose. That's not going to get you peace! Remember, Jesus said that He didn't give peace the way the world gives it. It's not about emptying yourself; it's about filling yourself with Jesus. It's the Person of Jesus and walking in the Spirit that brings peace.

In other words, you can copy the framework of faith without the Spirit, but it won't bear the same fruit. The point is, faith gets you in the Spirit, and that realm of consciousness is far greater and higher than the realm of the flesh.

The flesh is a limited realm—limited to man's strength. It's when we depend on what we can do instead of what God can do in us and through us. Faith gives you access to the Spirit of God where *all things are possible.* Yield yourself to the Holy Spirit. Paul talked about this in Galatians 3:3–5—

> Are you so foolish? Having begun in the Spirit, are you now being made perfect by the flesh? Have you suffered so many things in vain—if indeed it was in vain?

> Therefore, He who supplies the Spirit to you and works miracles among you, does He do it by the works of the law, or by the hearing of faith?

And again, in Romans 8:5–6—

> For those who live according to the flesh set their minds on the things of the flesh, but those who live according to the Spirit, the things of the Spirit. For to be carnally minded is death, but to be spiritually minded is life and peace.

The mission of anxiety is to get you distracted and in the flesh. Faith, however, gets you in the Spirit and tuned into the "all things are possible" network where the result is life and peace. In faith—believing God—it's possible to not be anxious about anything.

As we'll see, prayer and thanksgiving pave the way for this "faith focus" which allows you to rise above and see things more clearly.

Don't Stop Coming

Then Paul, giving the how-to application, says, "But in everything by prayer and supplication, with thanksgiving, let your requests be made known to God." I like how the NLT puts it:

> "Don't worry about anything; instead, pray about everything."

I remember coming in to 2008 with a vibrant prayer life. But when the fear and anxiety seemingly came out of nowhere, it felt like my strength was sapped. Depression had worked really hard to get me down, and I found myself dragging to get to prayer. Not because my love for God had waned. I was just really discouraged by the battle I was facing.

Assuming you're reading this book because you want peace, you probably know exactly what I'm talking about. Depression, fear, anxiety, heartache, shame, and the like can hinder our passion for prayer. Proverbs 15:13 says "By sorrow of the heart the spirit is broken." Some of you may be like Hannah in 1 Samuel 1, who never turned away from the place of prayer while she was in pain (which is a great example to follow). But for others, prayer has been somewhat avoided or neglected.

There could be tons of reasons why we neglect the place of prayer. The disappointment is too heavy, the fears have seemingly crippled you, the anxiety has completely distracted you, heartache has literally broken your spirit, or shame is lying to you and telling you that you're not good enough to approach God.

But I have to say this loud and clear:

DON'T STOP COMING!

Don't stop coming to the place of prayer. It's an atmosphere. It's the Presence of God that allows us to think straight and brings clarity. No matter what you feel, don't stop coming to the place of prayer. Do whatever it takes to get there. Come in faith. Keep putting your face in His face. Look at the character of God. Make your requests before Him and thank Him.

In speaking of King Rehoboam, king of Judah, the scriptures say "He did evil because he had not set his heart on seeking the Lord" (2 Chronicles 12:14 NIV). He did evil—not because he set his heart on evil, not because his parents were bad people, not because his circumstances were full of idolatry—Rehoboam did evil because he didn't set his heart on seeking the Lord. He neglected the place of prayer. He lacked the heavenly atmosphere.

Outside the atmosphere of God's presence there's the sway. That's what Rehoboam got caught up in. 1 John 5:19 says, "We know that we are of God, and the whole world lies under the sway of the wicked one." It's an entire world system that is in direct opposition to God. Without setting our hearts to seek the Lord, we risk getting caught up in the sway.

Just like salmon have it in their nature to swim upstream rivers and leap up waterfalls, Christians have it in their nature to go against the current of the world and its ways. But when we neglect the place of prayer, we risk getting caught up in the sway and we relinquish our supernatural heritage and identity.

The place of prayer, however, positions you for the mindset of Christ.

Paul, in telling us how to get to peace, said, in *everything*—through prayer, supplication, and thanksgiving—let your requests be made known to God. In everything. Don't stop coming.

Come to God.

Come humbly. Come sincerely. Come gratefully. Come expectantly. Come boldly.

> "Let us therefore come boldly to the throne of grace, that we may obtain mercy and find grace to help in time of need" (Hebrews 4:16).

> "And so, dear brothers and sisters, we can boldly enter heaven's Most Holy Place because of the blood of Jesus" (Hebrews 10:19 NLT).

Jesus qualified you to come. Whatever you do, just *don't stop coming.*

TAKE HIS PEACE, NOT HIS PLACE

During the encounter I had, I was lying on the ground while Jesus stood guard. I was in a position of rest and He was in a position of war. It would've been foolish for me to switch roles and have Him rest while I fight (remember the disciples on the boat?). Yet, in essence, that's what we do when we neglect the place of prayer; we take His place! It's time to rest and receive the peace of God.

Solomon said it like this: "Unless the Lord builds the house, those who build it labor in vain. Unless the Lord watches over the city, the watchman stays awake in vain. It is in vain that you rise up early and go late to rest, eating the bread of anxious toil; for he gives to his beloved sleep" (Ps. 127:1–2 ESV).

God created the sabbath as a blessing for man. (I look at sabbath twofold: 1) take a day of rest every week; 2) rest every day in what Christ has accomplished for you). I remember my pastor saying that when he skipped a day of rest, sometimes he'd end up getting sick. When he'd go to the Lord in prayer and ask what happened, the Lord would tell him, "You think you're bigger than Me?" Even God rested on the seventh day; and Jesus slept on the boat!

You need to rest. It's vain to wear yourself out thinking

that you're in charge of it all. God gives His beloved sleep! Charles Spurgeon said, "Often, when we have been fretting and worrying, we should have glorified God far more had we literally gone to sleep."[25] Taking a sabbath rest communicates far more trust in God than the vainness of anxiously toiling night and day.

Psalm 46:10 says, "Cease striving and know that I am God" (NASB95). The footnote for the word "cease" says it could also be translated as, "let go, relax." Let go! Relax! Or we could say *rest.* And what is it that we need to know? That God is God and you are not (really good news). Don't try to take His job.

In other words, don't fight God's battles. It's the place of rest that activates the warring nature of the Prince of Peace. The saints in the Old Testament heard it like this: "The battle is not yours, but God's...You will not need to fight in this battle. Position yourselves, stand still and see the salvation of the Lord, who is with you" (2 Chron. 20:15, 17). It's taking your cares, requests, and burdens to God in prayer and letting Him deal with what you can't. Know that He is God and enjoy His Presence. Worship Him and sing praise to Him.

I love what Isaiah prophesied regarding this: "Sing to the Lord a new song, and His praise from the ends of the earth."

Then God's response:

> The Lord shall go forth like a mighty man;
> He shall stir up His zeal like a man of war.
> He shall cry out, yes, shout aloud;
> He shall prevail against His enemies.
> —Isaiah 42:10, 13

That's exactly what happened in 2 Chronicles 20:22 when King Jehoshaphat appointed the worshippers to go ahead of the army. "Now when they began to sing and to praise, the Lord set ambushes against the people of Ammon, Moab, and Mount Seir, who had come against Judah; and they were defeated." When you rest in Him, God fights for you.

If we're going to fight any battle it's going to be the battle of faith—to believe God. If we're going to strive for anything it's to enter into His rest (1 Tim. 6:12, Heb. 4:11). These are, essentially, the same thing. We fight the good fight of faith and strive to enter into His rest. Faith in God is a place of rest. The position of rest is a position of faith. It's being seated in heavenly places, far above every enemy, in a higher perspective and place of authority. As we've just seen, praise is a huge key in accessing this faith and rest.

- When we try to qualify ourselves by our own acts of righteousness, we take His place as the Lord of our righteousness.
- When we try to fight all the battles ourselves, we take His place as our Defender.
- When we exhaust ourselves in anxious toil, we take His place as our Provider.

The list could go on, but you get the point.

When we take His place, we become restless. But when we trust in Him, we become restful.

Don't take His place; take His peace.

Rest and Responsibility

You may be saying, "Rest just sounds irresponsible. Don't we have to do something? Isn't faith without works dead?" To be clear, resting is not passivity or laziness. Rest is a position of the heart. The place of rest is the place of trust. Trust in what God has promised. Trust in who God says you are. Rest in Christ comes from confidence in God.

Jesus slept on a boat in the middle of a life-threatening storm. It's the ultimate picture of rest. He wasn't absolving His responsibility; He was demonstrating trust in the Father. Rest is not the absence of responsibility but the presence of trust. It's a posture that says you actively trust the Father—all the while, carrying out your normal duties and responsibilities.

There are times when I'm ministering somewhere and I'm not entirely sure what I'm going to speak on. But then, in the middle of doing a menial task like brushing my teeth, God drops an entire message in my heart. The restful posture of my heart positioned me to receive. John Paul Jackson said, "Peace is the potting soil of revelation."

The Holy Spirit came on Pentecost in a place where they were all *sitting*. Sitting is a position of resting. Bill Scheidler comments how he pictures "the disciples standing and singing and kneeling and praying, and doing everything they could to 'bring the Holy Spirit down.' Finally, when they are exhausted of all their efforts, they 'sit down' and then the Holy Spirit comes."[26]

But again, just to be clear, it doesn't mean you don't do anything. The temple in the Old Testament illustrates this. In short, there were three main areas. The outer court, the inner court, and then the holy places. The outer areas had busyness and people all around. The further you went in, the fewer people there were as the functions became more intentional and sacred (priestly duties, sacrifices, etc.). Until you finally come into the deepest and most holy place, the Holy of Holies. This is where the Presence of God dwelt. It was the most holy and sacred space. It was utterly peaceful.

Paul tells us in the New Testament that we are the temple of God now (1 Cor. 3:16). The picture is this: busyness on the outside, while there is complete and utter peace on the inside. Rest is a posture of the heart. In other words, we keep our responsibility intact on the outside while maintaining holiness and peace on the inside. Rest on the inside while busyness is on the outside. While two people could be doing the same things on the outside, one could be restless and the other could be restful.

It's the posture, condition, and motive of the heart that makes all the difference. Are they working for something they already have? Are they taking the place of God? Or have they rested in the fact that they're already loved? Are they working *from* that place of being fully loved and accepted? Are they trusting God to do what only He can do? All of the "works" can look the same on the outside, but what really matters is what's going on in the heart. The posture of your heart determines the measure of God's peace you experience. The work part of our faith never goes away; what matters is *why* you're working.

Settle it on the inside that God is for you. Everything that Jesus bought for you on the cross is yours—forgiveness, freedom, acceptance. You're loved, you're chosen, you're called, you're free, you're complete in Him. Rest means that you're not working *for* something you already have. Rest means that you're working *from* the place of what Jesus accomplished for you at the cross. "I'm already loved. I have the smile of God on me! I'm not trying to prove anything—I'm just doing what my Father put me here to do!" Rest launches you to work hard in the kingdom.

True rest sets you up for a passionate pursuit of God and His promises coming to pass. Jesus opened the way to very Presence of God, but we still need to enter into what was made available for us! Regarding promises, God gave Israel the promised land and promised to go with them—but they still had to go and take what was theirs.

Whenever you feel like you stepped out of the place of rest, ask the questions: Am I working for something God already gave me for free in Jesus? Am I trusting what God has said about me?

Going back to the temple illustration, note that only the priests were allowed in the inner court and holy places. They were set apart for that function. In the same way, we have to limit who or what we let into the deeper parts of our lives. Put up a "no trespassing" sign and don't allow the contrary voices to come into your heart and mind. Instead, cast those voices down and cast your cares on the Lord.

(In fact, the status of the Most Holy Place determined the status of the entire nation of Israel. Again, painting a picture for our lives: When we have peace on the inside, we can handle the storm on the outside. A couple other ways to say it: You can handle the storm outside if you can calm the storm inside. What's going on inside of you directly affects how you deal with what's going on around you. I'm talking about being at rest within yourself so you can handle life adequately. This points to peace *with* God and the peace *of* God.)

Peter (the disciple who discovered the limitations of his own ambition and zeal vs. the unlimited power of the Holy Spirit working through Him) said to humble ourselves under the mighty hand of God, "casting all your care upon Him, for He cares for you" (1 Peter 5:7). Pride says I can do it in my own strength, but it also puts you in a position where you're taking God's place. Humility positions you for the supernatural empowerment of God. He doesn't need you to fight in the flesh, He wants to empower you with His Spirit. Let Him be who He wants to be in your life—Defender and Prince of Peace. God opposes the proud but gives grace to the humble.

So, we cast our cares upon Him in prayer. Psalm 55:22 says, "Cast your burden on the Lord, And He shall sustain you; He shall never permit the righteous to be moved." Talk to Him about whatever is going on; get it out of you. Give your cares to God and give Him thanks. Boldly ask God what you want. Declare His truth over your life. Make the exchange—your cares for God's peace. A good friend taught me years ago to literally throw your hands up as a faith act of throwing your cares on God.

Back to Philippians 4, Paul went on to say that after you pray, "the peace of God, which surpasses all understanding" would come. (There's another thing to add to our definition of peace: *it surpasses understanding.*) In my vision, it was the sword of peace that brought me to a place of rest.

This kind of peace is beyond what our minds can comprehend. It excels beyond, it's superior to and far greater than our understanding. Which is why, at first glimpse, Jesus sleeping on a boat in the middle of a storm is startling and somewhat offensive (if you're on that boat). It doesn't make natural sense.

It's a peace that says, "I should be freaking out right now, but I'm actually at rest. The storm may be raging around me, but God's peace has calmed the winds inside me. I trust in God."

Peace Stands Guard

Prayer activates the peace of God that guards. Paul finally says that "the peace of God, which surpasses all understanding, will *guard* your hearts and minds through Christ Jesus."

The fierce nature of God's peace was painted well in the vision of the Lord dressed in samurai armor and standing guard with drawn sword. It's been said that a picture is worth a thousand words. If the Lord showed me a vision of Him dressed as a samurai, then there's probably something about samurai He wanted to communicate to me about Himself. By definition, samurai means "those who serve."[27] They were warriors who fought and served with dignity and honor.

Their main weapon and symbol was the sword they carried. Yet, the sword the Lord carried in my vision wasn't a samurai sword, it was more like a medieval times sword that was double edged. That speaks to me of the power of God's Word (see Heb. 4:12, Eph. 6:17, Rev. 1:16). Not only that, but it was said of the samurai that "the sword was the soul of a warrior."[28] I saw the sword of peace—which speaks to me that the peace that Jesus carried *within* manifested as a weapon. Peace was the weapon He used to defend me.

This isn't a passive, push-over version of Jesus that the world tries to portray. This is the Warring Prince of Peace who comes and stands guard over your heart and mind. Jesus is meek, but meekness does not equal weakness. Meek means strength under control. He dealt with what needed to be dealt with without losing his cool.

David called God his shepherd (Ps. 23:1). What's interesting, however, was that David was also a shepherd. After King Saul said that he was unqualified to fight Goliath, David responded by describing how he killed a lion and a bear while protecting his father's sheep:

> David said to Saul, "Your servant has been keeping his father's sheep. When a lion or a bear came and carried off a sheep from the flock, I went after it, struck it and rescued the sheep from its mouth. When it turned on me, I seized it by its hair, struck it and killed it. Your servant has killed both the lion and the bear; this uncircumcised Philistine will be like one of them, because he has defied the armies of the living God."
>
> —1 Sam. 17:34–36 NIV

If that's how David functioned as a shepherd, what do you think his image of God was when he said, "The Lord is my shepherd"? A passive push-over or a *fierce protector?*

The Greek word for "guard" means to protect by a military guard in order to prevent a hostile invasion.[29] The Amplified Bible translated it as a *garrison*: a body of troops stationed in a fortified place.[30] He's fierce against the enemies of your peace. He stands guard to prevent the hostile invasions of fear, anxiety, depression, shame, and the like. You may have been held captive by the mouth of the lion or bear of those enemies—but your Prince of Peace, the greater Son of David, is here to enforce the victory of His cross in your life and set you free.

Peace is a weapon. When the storms rage around you, vying for your attention, you use the weapon of peace to overcome. You stay in rest. You stay in peace. You don't let the storm around you become the storm within you.

No wonder why Jesus said, "Don't ever call My peace passive." Peace isn't submissive to the voice of the enemy—it pushes it back and shuts it down. It doesn't tolerate evil. Don't tolerate the voices of the enemy; don't even give them a chance at all—shut them down immediately. Do not allow them to have a voice in your life. It's the God of *peace* that *crushes* Satan under your feet (Romans 16:20). You need to know that you're not alone in the fight and that God is fighting for you. And if God is for you, who can be against you?

Jesus, the Warring Prince of Peace, wants to stand guard over you.

IT'S A HEART POSTURE

Activating the peace that guards doesn't only happen in a prayer room. In the vision, I was lying on the ground while Jesus stood guard. But I don't believe that God is saying we have to lay on the ground and rest every single time anxiety comes knocking at our door. Prayer and rest are a posture of the heart. The vision is a picture of what can happen in your heart wherever you go and in whatever situation you are in.

Applying this heart posture is one of the ways that prayer becomes a way of life, not just a place you visit. It's praying without ceasing—an open communication with God 24/7 (1 Thess. 5:17). It's living in such a way that you trust in the Lord, not in the circumstance. You've made the exchange of your cares for His peace. You've lifted up prayers, requests, and thanksgiving. And in that posture, the peace that guards is activated.

Take time to cultivate this heart posture regularly in your life. You can use the prayer and activation below as a guide. As you put the time in, this posture will become like second nature. The Prince of Peace is here to fight for you!

A PRAYER TO GET YOU THERE

Lord Jesus, Prince of Peace, I come to You now. I cast my cares on You and trust You to do for me what I cannot do for myself. Thank You that You fight for me and stand guard over me. I receive Your peace now, in Jesus' name. Amen.

ACTIVATION

Find a place of prayer where you can lay on your back. Give your cares to God in prayer and then declare His promises over your life and thank Him. Take a few minutes to rest in His Presence.

— 6 —

ACTIVATE!

Now may the God of peace Himself sanctify you completely; and may your whole spirit, soul, and body be preserved blameless at the coming of our Lord Jesus Christ.
—1 Thessalonians 5:23

My wife and I love to watch HGTV. It started when we were on the hunt for our first house but continues on even after our second home. If you're not familiar with it, HGTV is a network on television that has tons of shows on house renovation and buying/selling homes.

One of the things that is always amazing to see is the "before" and "after" of a house renovation. The flooring, cabinets, countertops, paint, design, and landscaping that are all brand new and upgraded. And I'm pretty sure every time these renovations lead to an open concept design. One of the benefits of watching HGTV is that you get to relax on the couch and see the results of someone's hard work. But *someone* had to put in the work!

The point is, if you're gonna walk in peace, you're gonna have to put in the work! You do your part and God does His. Although there have been plenty of applications up to this point, in this chapter, I'm giving twelve practical steps to take to activate God's peace in your life.

1. Renew your mind

"Do not be conformed to this world, but be transformed by the renewing of your mind" (Romans 12:2). I've been alluding to this the entire book. Replacing the lies of fear, anxiety, and shame with the truth of God's Word. The greatest way to renew your mind is by training it to think God's thoughts.

When the scripture said to be transformed by the renewing of your mind, the original word for "renewing" means renovation. It's a renewal; a complete change for the better.[31] It's HGTV in your thinking!

Here's some practical steps to take to renew your mind:

a. **Reject** the thoughts that are contrary to what God says in His Word (2 Cor. 10:4–5). Break agreement with any ungodly thought patterns.

b. **Replace** thoughts with truth.

- What does God say about that particular area of your life?
- Find scripture to stand upon.

c. **Rehearse** the truth.

- Meditate on the scripture.
- Memorize the scripture.
- Speak it out loud in first person.

"This Book of the Law shall not depart from *your mouth,* but you shall meditate in it day and night, that you may observe to do according to all that is written in it. For then you will make your way prosperous, and then you will have good success" (Joshua 1:8, emphasis mine). This is like when the *Property Brothers* are doing a renovation on a house and they come up against some rotted wood hidden behind the painted walls. They pull the bad stuff out and replace it with brand new lumber. You need new thoughts, God-thoughts, to replace the old rotten ways of thinking.

I remember the Lord speaking to me and helping me overcome unhealthy thought patterns—which I believe is also a word for those reading this book. He said, "You need to change the way you think about it...You're letting your past define you instead of Me."

Make no mistake: this kind of work is warfare.

> Though we live in the world, we do not wage war as the world does. The weapons we fight with are not the weapons of the world. On the contrary, they have divine power to demolish strongholds. We demolish arguments and every pretension that sets itself up against the knowledge of God, and we take captive every thought to make it obedient to Christ.
>
> —2 Corinthians 10:3–5 NIV

One of our greatest weapons is the Word of God. In fact, the Word is spoken of as a hammer that breaks a rock into pieces (Jer. 23:29). That sounds like divine power to demolish strongholds! We use the hammer of His Word to break down strongholds and say:

"That's not what God says, THIS is what God says, and THIS is truth! I believe what God says."

2. Get in the Word

This goes without saying, especially in light of the last point. But look at this verse:

> "Great peace have those who love Your law,
> And nothing causes them to stumble" (Psalm 119:165).
>
> "There is such a great peace and well-being that comes to the lovers of your Word, and they will never be offended" (Psalm 119:165 TPT).

Great peace! Right there—you get to insert every definition given in this book for what peace is.

A couple tips to help in this:

- Approach the Word with prayer
    - Ask the Holy Spirit to open your eyes to see (Ps. 119:18).
- Spend consistent time in the scripture.
    - This gives the Holy Spirit a "file cabinet" in your heart to pull from and remind you of what Jesus has spoken to you (John 14:26).
- Look for the *rhema*.
    - Jesus said in Matthew 4:4, "'Man shall not live by bread alone, but by every word *(rhema)* that proceeds from the mouth of God.'"

Rhema is a Greek word that, in short, speaks of the "now" word that God is highlighting to you. Although all of God's Word has supernatural life to it, the *rhema* comes with "now" power to strengthen you. What is God highlighting to you? What is He saying now? That's where your spiritual nutrients are! Right now!

The scripture is where you discover who God is, who you are, and what God says about your circumstances. It's where you have access to God's thoughts about whatever you're facing. God's Word gives us a higher reality to live from. Make time to devour the Word of God!

3. Pray for revelation

As discovered in the last chapter, prayer is a huge key to activating the peace of God. But this prayer is a pointed prayer: "That the God of our Lord Jesus Christ, the Father of glory, may give to you the spirit of wisdom and revelation *in the knowledge of Him*, the eyes of your understanding being enlightened" (Ephesians 1:17–18, emphasis mine).

And when this prayer is answered, peace is yours in abundance. There's something about knowing God in truth and purity that activates peace. Look at what Peter says: "Grace and *peace* be yours in abundance *through the knowledge* of God and of Jesus our Lord" (2 Peter 1:2 NIV, emphasis mine).

It's revelation knowledge. Revelation means you are seeing something that's always been there, but you couldn't see it until God opened your eyes. Pray Ephesians 1:17–18!

4. Repentance

Simply put, if there is known sin in your life, just repent. The ultimate peace we'll ever have is the peace that comes from knowing that we're right with God. This isn't to encourage you to go on a "witch hunt" and try to find everything wrong with you, but if you know there are things you're doing that are wrong in God's eyes, stop it. It's probably a big reason why you're experiencing a lack of peace.

> Search me, O God, and know my heart;
> Try me, and know my anxieties;
> And see if there is any wicked way in me,
> And lead me in the way everlasting.
>
> —Psalm 139:23–24

Notice how David said that God was doing the searching. Let the Holy Spirit convict you and repent accordingly. Don't listen to the voice of condemnation. It never helps you; it only makes the situation worse. Trust the Holy Spirit and the goodness of God.

For clarity, repentance means to change the way you think about something and to turn from sin. It's when we begin to think how God thinks about sin and we turn from it. Once you repent and confess to God, accept His gift of forgiveness and cleansing and move on (1 John 1:9). Don't let guilt or shame drive the narrative. Jesus' blood is more than enough to wash us clean and make us free.

Repentance speaks of turning from not only the actions that are unpleasing to God and unhealthy to us—it's changing the thought patterns that direct us in ways that contradict faith and the truth of God.

5. Forgiveness

One of the ways being a peacemaker comes into play is reconciling relationships. If there are people you are at odds with, chances are that broken relationship is acting as a peace-stealer in your life. I'm not talking about staying in an abusive or hostile relationship (which would require you to walk away and create healthy boundaries); I'm talking about acknowledging the fractions in relationships that we all experience from time to time and working to fix them.

Paul says in Romans 12:18 (NIV), "If it is possible, as far as it depends on you, live at peace with everyone." Jesus said with God all things are possible, but Paul said with people "*if* it is possible."

He's pointing to the fact that there's a chance it may not work to be at peace with everyone—but you can still do your part. Hence the phrase "as far as it depends on you." Then in verse 21 he says, "Do not be overcome by evil, but overcome evil with good." One of the greatest ways to overcome evil with good is to forgive.

Jesus tells a parable in Matthew 18:21–35 about the dangers of unforgiveness. In short, one man who is forgiven an enormously impossible debt goes out and throws into prison someone who owed him a much smaller payable debt. The one who forgave him the impossible-to-pay-off debt found out about it and this is what Jesus said:

> "In a fury of anger, the king turned him over to the prison guards to be tortured until all his debt was repaid.

> In this same way, my heavenly Father will deal with any of you if you do not release forgiveness from your heart toward your fellow believer."
>
> —Matthew 18:34–35 TPT

Unforgiveness opens the door to the "torturers." We'd all agree that the torturers are enemies of peace. Holding unforgiveness will definitely fracture relationships, but it will specifically hinder your own personal life. It's been said many times that unforgiveness is like drinking poison and expecting the other person to die. It really affects *you* in a negative way. Forgiveness doesn't mean that what the other person did was right. It means you're just not letting it control you anymore.

The ultimate reason we forgive is because God forgave us. "Bear with each other and forgive one another if any of you has a grievance against someone. Forgive as the Lord forgave you." (Col. 3:13). You may want to take a moment and think about the cross of Christ and what He did for you there. We surely didn't deserve His love and forgiveness, but He gave it anyway. That's good news!

This could be the topic of an entire book itself. But here's the question: Is there anyone that you need to forgive? Take a moment and ask the Holy Spirit if there's anyone you need to forgive.

If He shows you anyone, or anyone comes to mind, take the right step and forgive them. When I'm ministering to people in this area, I usually lead them in a simple prayer like this:

> Lord Jesus, because You forgive me, I choose to forgive______________________________
> for________________________________.

Let them go, release them to God, and stop holding it against them. It's time to move on with your life. Forgiveness is the key to freedom from the prison of offense. Forgiveness makes you inaccessible to the torture of bitterness. This just might be your key to accessing the peace of God.

6. Community

We need people! I'm talking about our spouses, children, family, friends, church family, and leaders. Proverbs 18:1 says, "A man who isolates himself seeks his own desire; he rages against all wise judgment." In other words, we miss out on the healthy and helpful perspective of others when we isolate ourselves.

As we've seen, the importance of being in the presence of people has been challenged in recent times. Not only that, anxiety and depression, many times, causes lethargy toward connection with others.

The truth is, you don't see everything. People can help to give you clarity about a blind spot you have or give you helpful feedback about what they see in your life. Talk to someone you trust or find a godly counselor. Let someone else help give you clarity and allow them to speak into your life. Let them share insights from their lives and how they've overcome.

I'm not talking about "Job's friends" or even people who just tell you what you want to hear. I'm talking about people who will love and encourage you, not be afraid to tell you the truth, and who will direct you in a Christ-like way.

Bottom line is, we need people to tell us truth and to encourage us. We need people to pray for us. We need people to prophesy to us. We need people to just have fun with and get our minds off the drama. This will actually help calm the storm inside of us. We need people!

7. Focus

> "You will keep him in perfect peace,
> Whose mind is stayed on You,
> Because he trusts in You."
>
> —Isaiah 26:3

Direct your thoughts toward God. Again, this is one that's been alluded to throughout the book. When the swirl of fear tries to get you caught up in its winds, focus on the One who's seated above it all. He sits in the heavens and laughs. Rest in the One who rested in the storm.

Philippians 4 says, right after our anchor passage:

> Finally, brethren, whatever things are true, whatever things are noble, whatever things are just, whatever things are pure, whatever things are lovely, whatever things are of good report, if there is any virtue and if there is anything praiseworthy—meditate on these things.
>
> —Philippians 4:8

The word for meditate in the original language means to "take an account of."

It's like the old phrase "count your blessings."

I love how the ESV footnote connects verses 8–9: "Think about these things—which things you have also learned and received and heard and seen in me—practice these things, and the God of peace will be with you." He connects the "these things" in verse 8 to the "these things" that they've seen exemplified in him and received from his ministry. They had a living example.

Paul says essentially, "Take my lead on this. I've disciplined my life to keep the good things in the forefront. I consistently put to remembrance the testimonies of God, the word of the Lord, and all the life-giving things I know of. You've seen me live this out and you've received from my ministry. I've discovered that when I do this, the God of peace is present with me. And if you follow my example, you'll experience Him too."

Direct your thoughts toward good. Whatever you focus on you empower. If you find yourself with a lack of peace, take your eyes off the negative and shift your focus on God and the good. You may be surprised at how much God *is* doing and how much good *is* happening all around you.

8. Praise & worship

One of the best ways to shift your focus is through praise and worship! When you're singing praise, you're directing your focus on who God is and what He's done. We praise Him because He's worthy and He's given us mercy.

Think about that. Think about the things He's done for you; where He's brought you from; how you've encountered Him; how He's changed your life; all that He did at the cross and resurrection; all that He did in your family; all that He did in your finances; all that He did in your ministry! It's like the old Pentecostal song, "When I think of His goodness..." You don't even have to sing for it to be praise—you can shout, you can dance, you can declare, you can run!

> "Enter into His gates with thanksgiving,
> And into His courts with praise.
> Be thankful to Him, and bless His name."
>
> —Psalm 100:4

Then look up and see who He is. He is Alpha and Omega, He is the Beginning and the End, He is Almighty God, He is Servant of all, He is the Lion of Judah, He is the Lamb that was slain, He's the Prince of Peace, the King of Kings, the Savior of the world, the God of all grace, the Holy One of Israel, our Apostle, our High Priest, Creator, Provider, Healer, Father, Mighty God, Son of God, Son of man, Friend, Hope, Life, Lord of glory...He is JESUS!

The perpetual fires of worship are fueled by perpetually beholding God. True worship is birthed out of seeing God. Look to Him again and fuel your worship.

That really is enough to praise God. But how does this specifically relate to peace? Look at this verse—

> "One generation shall praise Your works to another, and shall declare Your mighty acts."
> —Psalm 145:4

The word for praise is the Hebrew word is *shabach.* It means to address in a loud tone, but it also means to soothe, or pacify.[32] In short, to proclaim and to pacify. This kind of praise has a twofold expression—God is being praised and your heart is being pacified.

Don't hold back your praise! Bless God with a loud voice and watch as He supernaturally calms your soul.

What's more is Psalm 149 speaks about the power of the high praises of God. This is the joyful and exuberant praise. When we engage in that type of praise, the enemy is bound in chains. i.e., your anxiety gets bound up and you can think clearly again.

It's time to praise God!

9. Pray in tongues

> "He who speaks in a tongue edifies himself" (1 Cor. 14:4).

Here's the renovation again! The word for "edifies" means to build a house.[33] When you pray in tongues, you are building yourself up spirit, soul, and body. It's honestly one of the best ways to strengthen yourself in the Lord. The Holy Spirit prays with your spirit and prays perfect prayers through you; exactly what you need to pray.

One of the things that's great about tongues is that your natural mind doesn't understand it. That should get you used to the peace that *surpasses* understanding!

Praying in tongues gives you access to the mind of God. Romans 8:6 says, "For to be carnally minded is death, but to be *spiritually minded is life and peace*" (emphasis mine). When your mind is running rampant with fearful thoughts, praying in the Spirit gives you a tune up to the mind that is life and peace. Instead of letting fear rule you, you take dominion back and rule yourself under the Lordship of Jesus. The Holy Spirit lifts you up above the carnal mind into the mind of Christ—the One who sleeps in the storm.

I remember when a group of friends led a guy in the baptism of the Holy Spirit, and he received the gift of tongues. He started speaking Mandarin Chinese. One of the guys who was there was actually a missionary in China for six years, so he understood what he was saying. In Chinese, he kept repeating, "You believe in Him! You believe in Him!"

I believe it was 1 Corinthians 14:28—"But if there is no interpreter, let him keep silent in church, and let him speak to himself and to God." In short, I believe that if the tongue is horizontal (to people) then it needs to be interpreted. If it's vertical (to God), then it doesn't need an interpretation because, hello, God understands it! So, when Paul is saying to keep silent in the church, he's saying don't speak in tongues to a group of people if you don't have an interpretation. Not because it's a horrendous sin (which it definitely is not), but because it wouldn't help anyone if they didn't understand.

But he goes on to say, let him speak to himself and to God; which tells me that you can still speak in tongues in church if you don't have an interpreter, just don't address people—address yourself and God. I was saying all that to get to this point—we'd all agree that speaking in tongues is a supernatural way to pray to God, but Paul also says that we are speaking to ourselves!

Back to the testimony of the young man speaking Chinese, I believe he was prophesying to himself, by the unction of the Holy Spirit, to believe in God. I believe many times when we pray in tongues, we are actually speaking the word of the Lord to ourselves. The Holy Spirit is flowing through us to speak exactly what we need to receive from the Lord—and *that* builds us up.

I recommend setting aside time every day to pray in tongues. "But you, beloved, building yourselves up on your most holy faith, praying in the Holy Spirit" (Jude 20).

(If you haven't started flowing in this gift yet, Jesus said it's available to you [Mark 16:17]. Stop and ask Him right now to baptize you with His Holy Spirit and give you the gift of tongues. Then open your mouth and start speaking. For more on this, see Appendix 3.)

10. Fasting

> "When you fast..." (Matthew 6:16).

Fasting is one of the most powerful weapons we have as believers. Jesus taught that fasting was a part of the normal Christian life. He didn't say "*if* you fast," He said, "*when* you fast."

I won't do an entire study on fasting here, but I highly recommend Jentezen Franklin's book *Fasting* for great teaching, revelation, and testimonies on this subject.

In defining fasting, Jentezen Franklin said, "Fasting is refraining from food for a spiritual purpose." And to be clear, it's not just a hunger strike.

Fasting is to be coupled with prayer.

Here are a few quick benefits of fasting:

- Your relationship with God is strengthened.
- You get spiritually sharpened.
- Your flesh gets put in check.
- You see supernatural breakthrough.

In my experience, fasting and prayer helps me immensely to breakthrough when the mental noise and anxiety won't seem to fade. It does what David said in Psalm 27:6— "Then my head will be exalted above the enemies who surround me." Join fasting and prayer with praying in tongues and praise, thanksgiving, and worship and you've got a recipe for explosive supernatural breakthrough!

Jesus went on to say, "And your Father who sees in secret will reward you openly" (Matthew 6:18).

11. Presence

It's His Presence that changes everything. He *is* peace.

I'm not talking about a mental acknowledgement that God is with you. I'm talking about the manifest Presence of God; when He walks in the room; when His anointing destroys every yoke of oppression; when He pours out His love into our hearts; when His Spirit reminds us of who we are and who He is; when He draws near.

You might want to pause right now, open your hands, close your eyes, and pray, "Holy Spirit, come."

The psalmist was wrestling with why the wicked seemed to prosper and he said, "When I tried to understand it all, I just couldn't. It was too puzzling—too much of a riddle to me. But then one day I was brought into the sanctuaries of God, and in the light of glory, my distorted perspective vanished. Then I understood that the destiny of the wicked was near!" (Ps. 73:16–17 TPT). It was the manifest Presence of God that changed everything!

Seek His face. Pursue His Presence.

12. Have fun!

> "A merry heart does good, like medicine" (Proverbs 17:22).

> "A joyful, cheerful heart brings healing to both body and soul" (Proverbs 17:22 TPT).

What do you do for fun?

What makes your heart happy?

When's the last time you did something just for fun?

It's time to get off your smart phone and social media. I commission you: Go have fun! Smile! Laugh!

Conclusion

These points may seem overly simple—but they all point back to maintaining your relationship with God in practical ways. This is what it's all about. Yes, there are other practical methods to cultivate peace, like counseling, exercise, diet, and getting enough sleep. I won't dive into those in this book, but they're worth looking into.

Ultimately, peace is an inside job. These steps are not to be legalistically applied. They're here to, yes, release peace, but ultimately strengthen your relationship with God—who *is* peace.

Approach them that way. Not as rigorous to-dos, but as ways to grow closer to God and obtain what He's made available for you to have—and as we've seen, *wants* you to have.

ACTIVATION

Take at least three of these practical steps and implement them into your daily life.

— 7 —

BACK ON TRACK

You did not receive the spirit of slavery leading again to fear, but you received the Spirit of adoption, by whom we cry, "Abba, Father."
—Romans 8:15 NET

As we've all seen, the world changed in March 2020. The COVID-19 pandemic officially hit and literally impacted everyone on the planet…and governments are still figuring out how to lead going forward. I've had friends get it and experience effects that range from very mild and easy to cope with to being out for months and facing debilitating depression. But although the disease is real and people have been adversely affected by it, I propose that the greater pandemic is a pandemic of fear.

When you see people walking down the street outside, looking like they're about to face a zombie apocalypse based on the hazmat suit they're wearing, you can't help but think the real problem is inside their heads and not in the world. People have a mask *and* a face shield while they're walking their dog *outside* and *no one* is around.

Maybe they just have raging allergies and it has nothing to do with the pandemic; either way, it goes to show that the enemy they're facing isn't really the virus.

I'm pretty sure it's *fear.*

Fear has a way of crippling people and hindering them from real life. It's a thief that steals people's ability to be fully present. It holds people back from what they were created to do. It works to restrain them from their God-given destiny.

But when God has His way in our hearts, the peace of God sets us free and we're able to run freely into His plans for our lives. Where fear would sideline us, the peace of God gets us back on track.

DEFEATING THE ENEMY WITHIN

I'm a fan of The Chronicles of Narnia series by C.S. Lewis and while the movies don't always do the greatest job following the narrative of the books, I still like watching them. In *The Voyage of the Dawn Treader* movie, the magician who helps the kids find their way lets them know that they are all about to be tested. But he gives them a key to overcome. He says, "To defeat the darkness out there, you must defeat the darkness inside yourself." He points to the fact that the real battle is *internal.*

I alluded to this back in Chapter 4 when I said we need to learn how to calm the storm inside of us so we can handle the storms around us. If you can defeat the enemy within, you can handle any enemy outside. In fact, I propose that the greater enemy you face isn't on the outside, it's on the inside. Let me explain.

I want to look at three stories in scripture that essentially tell the same story—

- David and Goliath – 1 Samuel 17
- Jesus sleeping in the storm – Mark 4:35–41
- The disciples locked in the upper room – John 20:19–29

In each story, the people of God were crippled by fear, and it hindered their God-given destiny. 1 Samuel 17:11 says the people of God were dismayed and greatly terrified. Why? Because they had listened to voice of the giant. We saw in Mark 4 that the disciples were freaked out because they listened to the voice of the storm. Then in John 20:19, the disciples were locked in a room because they were afraid the Jews were going to kill them the same way they did to Jesus.

Look what Romans 8:15 (NET) says: "For you did not receive the spirit of slavery leading again to fear, but you received the Spirit of adoption, by whom we cry, 'Abba, Father.'" I've always looked at this verse as talking about a spirit of fear, but that's not what it says. It says a spirit of *slavery* leads to fear. Slavery is when you submit to a master. You are slaves to the one whom you obey (see Rom. 6:16). Whoever you submit to determines your environment. Your master determines your environment.

When Jesus is our Master, we get the benefits of His environment, or kingdom—righteousness, peace, and joy in the Holy Spirit (Rom. 14:17). Our Master doesn't lead us to fear but to the Father. But in this case, the spirit of slavery leads to an environment to fear. In each story, the people of God submitted to the wrong voice, and it created their environment. To reiterate—Israel listened to Goliath, and they were crippled by fear. The disciples listened to the storm, and they were crippled by fear. The disciples later listened to the potential death threat of the Jews, and they were crippled by fear.

I've asked this before, but let's go again:

Whose voice are you listening to? Whose voice are you letting tell the story?

Whoever you submit to determines your environment. The disciples on the boat let the voice of the storm be their master. Yet, when they woke Jesus up, they called Him Master (Luke 8:24). He was Master with their mouths but not Master in their hearts! In that moment, they switched allegiances and got the fruit of their choice. They experienced the spirit of slavery that leads to fear.

Thank God that's not the Spirit He has for us. He gave us the spirit of adoption. We are welcomed into the family of God where we get to hear the voice of the Father speaking life and love over us! His voice crushes the contrary words and thoughts.

The greater enemy they all faced was actually within. One of the best keys to defeating the enemy within is outlined in James 4:7 (NIV): "Submit yourselves, then, to God. Resist the devil, and he will flee from you." Yield yourself to the voice of the Father.

Let's look at this a little deeper.

UNSEEN ENEMY

What's interesting to me is that in each story, the enemy moved deeper into the unseen realm. Israel faced a literal person. An ugly, giant, gangly looking guy who probably smelled pretty bad and could talk trash (my personal description). Then later, the disciples faced not a person but a storm. Then even further, when the disciples were locked in the upper room, they faced a threat.

Many times, we want to point the finger and say that our problems come from all these external factors. We'd like to blame our upbringing, our family, our boss, our leaders, our job, our bad relationships, and those things do have an impact on our lives—but at the end of the day, we have to take responsibility for where our lives are at. With the help of God, we can break free.

Israel could've pointed at the giant as their problem. But it was really the fact that they submitted to his taunting and let their hearts be filled with fear. The disciples could've said that the storm was their biggest problem. Don't get me wrong, water coming into your boat in the middle of a storm is a problem—but letting fear into your heart is a greater problem. You won't be able to face your problem adequately if fear is running the show. The disciples in the upper room could've said they were stuck because the threat of the Jews. But I propose they were stuck because of fear. In the Book of Acts, they couldn't care less about the threats they experienced, which tells me once the fear is dealt with, the mission goes on.

I said earlier that the greater, or real enemy, isn't on the outside—it's on the inside.

Goliath wasn't the real enemy—it was fear.

The storm wasn't the real enemy—it was fear.

The Jews weren't the real enemy—it was fear.

Jesus calmed the storm that threatened the death of the disciples, but the same disciples were afraid of death again when they were locked in the room.

In other words, He took the outside enemy away, but the inside enemy still remained—to prove that the outside enemy wasn't the real problem; it was fear on the inside. In fact, many times the outside enemy works to bring to the surface what was already there in the first place. The outside enemies are just pawns in the greater narrative of the grace of God to transform our lives. God uses Goliath to expose our greater need to be free on the inside. The greater enemy, the thing that hinders you, needs to be defeated on the inside.

CHANGE YOUR FILTER

When I was growing up, we had these photos people could take called Glamour Shots. People would go to the mall and get their pictures taken (girls with poofy bangs and guys with the gangster straight face) —then they would be edited to add this cloudy, glossy, '90s vibe to them.

When I was in junior high, people would bring these bad boys to school and pass the photos around like it was the coolest thing in town. If you're older, you know exactly what I'm talking about. If you're younger, don't be jealous. The fact is, back then we didn't have all the fancy filters y'all have on social media.

Nowadays, you can go on Instagram or Snapchat (if that's still a thing) and use filters that make your face look like a dog slurping with its tongue or put your own face on a Bernie Sanders meme. The point is, in the same way people use filters to alter the way they see themselves and others on social media, we all have internal filters that impact the way we see life.

I'll use a familiar phrase in a slightly different way: When the storm around you becomes the storm inside you, the storm becomes *the filter* through which you see life.

Remember the disciples had a distorted perception of what was going on in the boat and they accused Jesus of not caring about them. They thought they were going to die. They called Jesus "Master" even though they had submitted to another voice. There was a lot of distortion in their perception because the storm became their filter.

Remember, the real enemy is on the inside. But that doesn't mean that the outside enemies can't influence what happens on the inside. The space between the storm and your heart is where the warfare happens. *That* is the battleground. The adversary, the devil, wants the storm to get inside of you so it will hinder the way you see life. If the devil can get you to think like him, it'll distort your perception and you'll end up seeing like him.

Filters could be fear, anxiety, anger, offense, wounds, guilt, shame, and trauma. Praise God there's a way out!

One of the best ways to overcome a distorted filter is gratitude. Remember Philippians 4:6–7? One of the keys to prayer that leads to peace is *thanksgiving*. Don't get stuck on what you didn't have, be grateful for what you did have. Choose humility and gratitude instead of pride and entitlement. "Thank you" cleanses your lenses. You enter into the Presence of God from a place of gratitude, which provides the clarity you need to approach life from a healthy place. The good news is that for the rest of your life you'll always have something to be grateful for.

One of the things that is so powerful about when Jesus fed the 5,000+ with just five loaves of bread and two fishes was how He thanked God for the food that He did have. Imagine how potentially stressful that situation could have been! The plan was to feed the multitudes but all they had was a small lunch—and Jesus never complained about what He didn't have. He gave thanks for what they did have. The miraculous was launched from a place of thankfulness.

Is it possible that the "storm" has become your filter and that's why peace is lacking in your life? Regardless of the circumstances you find yourself in, take a few moments to thank God in prayer right now. Take off the wrong filters and put on the filter of gratitude.

VICTORY UNLEASHES WARRIORS

One of my favorite parts of the story of David and Goliath is what happens to Israel once David defeated the giant:

> David ran and stood over him. He took hold of the Philistine's sword and drew it from the sheath. After he killed him, he cut off his head with the sword.
>
> When the Philistines saw that their hero was dead, they turned and ran. Then the men of Israel and Judah *surged forward with a shout* and *pursued the Philistines* to the entrance of Gath and to the gates of Ekron.
>
> Their dead were strewn along the Shaaraim road to Gath and Ekron.
>
> When the Israelites returned from chasing the Philistines, *they plundered their camp.*
>
> —1 Samuel 17:51–53 NIV (emphasis mine)

Israel went from being crippled by fear to surging forward with a shout! The warrior nature inside of them was awakened and they chased the enemy off their land and plundered them.

Just like Israel, you were not made to be crippled by fear, you were made to fight! Once David killed Goliath, it set them free to do what they were made to do. They got back on track once they saw the victory. David's victory unlocked Israel. This is the effect of victory on a people crippled by fear—it provides the courage to *run and fight!*

I've talked about the fierce nature of the Prince of Peace, but the truth is, we're being transformed into His image! Jesus isn't the only one with armor—we have the armor of God! Armor isn't made for pacifists; it's made for warriors! The same way that David's victory unleashed the warriors in Israel, Jesus' victory at the cross and resurrection unleashes the church to be the fierce warriors we were created to be. It's in our nature. We weren't meant to be dominated; we were meant to take dominion. A war in front of you is meant to awaken the warrior within you.

We are the violent ones who take the kingdom by force! (Matt. 11:12). You know by now that the enemies aren't people but everything that stands in the way of the peace Jesus paid for us to have. We're full of compassion and kindness for people, but full of vengeance and violence for fear, shame, and all the others.

What does that fierceness look like?

When demons manifested in Jesus' ministry, He always silenced them. "But Jesus rebuked him, saying, 'Be quiet, and come out of him!'" "He did not allow the demons to speak, because they knew Him," "But He sternly warned them that they should not make Him known" (Mark 1:25, 34, 3:12). At first glance you may think, if they knew who He was, why shut them up? Their skewed view of Jesus would corrupt people's perceptions. Jesus refused to let the demons drive the narrative and paint the picture of who He was. When Jesus went about casting demons out, He was taking away their public voice.

Remember, peace is not passive. Jesus was shutting down the voice of the enemy. That's not passivity; that's taking dominion with the kingdom of God. Let me repeat what I said back in Chapter 5. Peace isn't submissive to the voice of the enemy. It doesn't tolerate evil; it pushes it back and shuts it down. Don't tolerate the voices of the enemy; don't even give them a chance at all—even if there is a little truth (the demons knew who Jesus was!). Shut them down immediately. Do not allow them to have a voice in your life. Lift up the shield of faith and quench the fiery darts of the enemy.

It's time for us to shake off fear and take possession the promises of God! We are meant to be warriors in the kingdom—kicking giants out of our promised land and taking back our God-given territory. The land of the Philistines was actually part of the promised land that God had given to Israel. It's interesting to note that the name Philistines means "immigrants."[34] An immigrant is defined as "a person who migrates to another country, usually for permanent residence."[35] I believe it's a picture of what the enemy does in our day: He tries to migrate into the promises of God for our lives and take up permanent residence. He wants to hinder us from fully experiencing the promises of God.

God told Israel that when they came into the promised land, they were to drive out the inhabitants and take possession of the land. If they didn't drive them out, the inhabitants would end up being "irritants in your eyes and thorns in your sides, and they shall harass you in the land where you dwell" (Num. 33:55). Years later, they still hadn't driven the Philistines out and they experienced the harassment God spoke of. The Lord told Joshua that there was "very much land yet to be possessed. This is the land that yet remains: all the territory of the Philistines" (Josh. 13:1–2).

Many times, we can do exactly what Israel did: tolerate the enemies possessing our promises. As a result, the harassment of anxiety and the like hinders us from fully experiencing God's promise. This is why I love that Israel, after seeing David's victory, got courage enough to stop tolerating the harassment of the enemy and chase them off their God-given territory! And they plundered them!

If the real enemy is within, the victory is also within! It's time to see Jesus' victory for you at the cross! See Him defeating your fear and shame. See Him washing away your sin. See Him demonstrating His love for you. See Him risen from the grave and stand up with Him in resurrection power! Don't allow the enemies we've been talking about to settle on your God-given promised land. Refuse them. Don't let fear take the place of the promise of Jesus' peace. Take courage and chase the enemy off of your promises!

I like how Jesus didn't say that He would move the

mountains, but that we, through the voice of faith, would speak to the mountains and they would move (Mark 11:22–23). Follow me on this, and let's look one more time at the story of Jesus sleeping on the boat. Mark 4:38 says that Jesus was asleep in the stern of the boat. The stern is the back of the boat away from the rudder, or steering wheel. One devotional said, "To be asleep at the wheel is negligent, but to be asleep in the stern is trusting."[36] Jesus was trusting the Father to get them all to the other side.

But as I look at this story, I can't help but think that Jesus was setting the disciples up to grow in faith. He wasn't asleep at the wheel; He was in the back of the boat! Which means He intentionally left the steering to someone else. Ultimately, he entrusted this task to the Father, but in a very practical way, the disciples were responsible as well. He was putting the disciples in charge. He was providing an opportunity for them to rise to the occasion. He was using this moment to awaken the warrior within.

Although it took them some time to "wake up" and develop their faith, when Jesus woke up at the cry of the disciples, He didn't ask His Father to stop the storm; He spoke to the wind and the waves and it calmed. My friend Jerame Nelson says, "The kingdom of God is voice activated." He showed them by example how to speak in faith. He showed them what a warrior in the kingdom looked like: not tolerating contrary voices and putting them in their place and speaking with authority.

James 3:4–5 says this: "Look also at ships: although they are so large and are driven by fierce winds, they are turned by a very small rudder wherever the pilot desires.

Even so the tongue is a little member and boasts great things." Jesus left the disciples at the steering wheel, or the *rudder*. James correlates the rudder with the tongue.

This was their chance to activate their God-given authority and speak! My friend Gary Zamora said, "They had enough faith to wake Him up, but not enough faith to speak like Him." Jesus left them at the steering wheel of their mouth! It's time to talk less *about* the storm and talk *to* the storm! Stop giving so much airtime to the storm and start talking about how great your God is. Let the sound of faith come forth!

Peace Be unto You

It's a bummer to end up locked in the "room of fear," but the good news is that is exactly where Jesus met His disciples. You have to know that if you're dealing with anxiety, that Jesus isn't outside the room waiting for you to get over your problem so you can get on with life. *He walks through the walls and meets you right there.*

Every time Jesus appears to His disciples after His resurrection and shows them His scars, He releases peace to them. In that day, peace, or shalom, would be a common way to greet one another, but I believe there was a greater meaning than a common greeting. He was declaring that He had just won the victory that destroyed the authority that binds to chaos. He was releasing peace to them.

In John 20:19–29, Jesus releases peace three times to His disciples. Each time He is speaking to a specific area that had hindered them. Peace was the answer to their hindrances.

1. Fear

"On the evening of that first day of the week, when the disciples were together, with the doors locked for fear of the Jewish leaders, Jesus came and stood among them and said, 'Peace be with you!'" (John 20:19 NIV).

As we've looked at, the disciples were locked in a room because of fear. Their prison of inward fear manifested in the outward room being locked. The first thing Jesus said to them was "*peace.*"

Because of the pandemic, people all around the world were locked in their homes. Some because of a mandatory request for safety, others because of fear. The latter is what we're addressing. You may not be locked up any more physically, but are you locked up mentally because of fear? The list could go on and on about what type of fear, but it's not relevant.

If fear has locked you up, Jesus wants to release peace in that area. Jesus' answer for debilitating fear is peace.

2. Unbelief

Thomas didn't happen to be there when Jesus appeared the first time. He didn't believe the testimony of the other disciples and said he wouldn't believe unless he saw Jesus' scars himself. Jesus came, supernaturally, into the room again and guess what His first word was—*peace.*

Jesus released peace into unbelief.

After Thomas encountered the Risen Christ himself, Jesus said to him,

> "Thomas, because you have seen Me, you have believed. Blessed are those who have not seen and yet have believed." (John 20:29)

Faith is a substance. There was a faith substance in the other's testimony of seeing Jesus. Thomas didn't accept it. Jesus said, essentially, "Listen, Thomas. It's not about seeing or not seeing. You can see and have the substance, or you can not see and have substance. It's not about seeing as much as it is about the substance."

Fear gives way to unbelief. But faith is always there waiting. Get the substance of faith.

3. Mission

When Jesus supernaturally walked in the room the first time, He showed them His scars and the disciples rejoiced. "So Jesus said to them again, 'Peace to you! As the Father has sent Me, I also send you'" (John 20:21). He spoke peace and then commissioned them.

If there's one thing a lack of peace does, it's gets you off mission. I'd say having the most qualified people to change the world for the kingdom of God locked in a room because of fear is a clear picture of "off mission." They couldn't fulfill their calling locked up in a room. They needed to break free and go forth!

In 2020, the church got thrown off track. Not necessarily because of the pandemic, racial tension, and political unrest, but because of her response to it. I don't presume to say that leading in a world pandemic is easy, but it felt like we got distracted. The new normal should be the church coming back to Jesus being the center of it all and His kingdom advancing. It's not that we don't address relevant issues, it's that we keep the main thing the main thing. Preach Jesus!

The point being, the warfare against you is to get you off mission. You were made for mission. Jesus releasing peace was directly tied to sending the disciples. The peace of God puts you back on track.

THE MISSION OF PEACE

Let's recap the definition of peace:

> Completeness, soundness, welfare, health, prosperity, tranquility, absence of agitation, and contentment. It means wholeness—nothing missing, nothing broken. It's unshakeable and victorious. It settles the anxious heart. It surpasses understanding. Peace is one third of the kingdom of God and a fruit of the Holy Spirit.
>
> It's rooted in a Person, not a circumstance. It's part of the nature of God. It's God's order, vibrant harmony, and freedom from chaos. Peace is a Fierce Protector.

All of this is God's will for your life. It's no wonder that David wrote that one of the keys to loving life and seeing good days was to seek peace and pursue it (Ps. 34:14). But it doesn't end there. Peace puts you back on track. Peace has a mission.

When Paul wrote about the armor of God, he wrote about what would be put on your feet: "and with your feet fitted with the readiness that comes from the gospel of *peace*" (Eph. 6:15 NIV, emphasis mine). Thayer's Greek Lexicon explains the original word for "readiness" as "with the promptitude and alacrity which the gospel produces."[37] Alacrity can be defined as brisk and cheerful eagerness and readiness. Alacrity means you're ready to go!

Notice that this alacrity comes from the gospel *of peace.* We receive peace with God through Christ as we've received His forgiveness, repented, and made Jesus Lord of our lives. We receive all that Jesus paid to give us at the cross. The peace of God puts our lives back in order, destroys chaos in our lives, and we learn to rest in Jesus as He fights for us. Regardless of circumstances, we can live in His unshakeable peace. Out of *that* place, we are freed up to run into our God-given destiny. We put on the gospel of peace and we have a cheerful and brisk eagerness to go after what we're put on earth for. We come alive when we're back on mission and doing what God created us to do.

Peace truly puts you back on track. Jesus wants to give you peace so you can have a quality life and fulfill His plan for your life. You have a unique contribution to the world! Don't let fear steal it from you; pursue peace and fulfill God's will!

A Prayer to Get You There

Lord, thank You that You've defeated every enemy at the cross! Enforce Your victory in my life today. I receive Your peace and I will run into Your plans for me. I know You made me to reign in life and walk in peace. Let Your viewpoint become mine. Thank You for freedom in Christ!

CONCLUSION

LET PEACE RULE

Let the peace of God rule in your hearts, to which also you were called in one body; and be thankful.
—Colossians 3:15

Walking in God's peace is not a one and done, it's way of life. You don't just pray once and never feel anxiety again.

It's learning how to cast our cares on God, so that the next time anxiety flies at us it just rolls off us like water off a duck's back.

- It's trusting God and resting in the fact that He's moving.
- It's believing God regardless of what you see.
- It's thanking Him in every circumstance.

In the passage above, the Greek word for "rule" is "to be an umpire." An umpire is defined as: "a person selected to rule on the plays in a game."[38] In other words, the umpire calls the shots. What he says goes! What he lets happen is allowed to happen. What he doesn't let happen isn't allowed to happen. He is the filter through which everything has to go.

Paul said to let the peace of God be that umpire in your heart.

- Don't let fear tell your story.
- Don't let anxiety cripple you the rest of your life.
- Don't let the storms around you become the storms inside you.

But rather let, allow, give place to, yield to: *Let* the peace of God call the shots. Draw from the life of Jesus.

Peace will do its work if we do ours.

APPENDIX 1

SCRIPTURES ON PEACE

For meditation, declaration, application, and study

"Be anxious for nothing, but in everything by prayer and supplication, with thanksgiving, let your requests be made known to God; and the peace of God, which surpasses all understanding, will guard your hearts and minds through Christ Jesus" (Philippians 4:6–7).

"I know the thoughts that I think toward you, says the Lord, thoughts of peace and not of evil, to give you a future and a hope" (Jeremiah 29:11).

"I have told you these things, so that in me you may have peace. In this world you will have trouble. But take heart! I have overcome the world" (John 16:33 NIV).

"Come to me, all you who are weary and burdened, and I will give you rest. Take my yoke upon you and learn from me, for I am gentle and humble in heart, and you will find rest for your souls. For my yoke is easy and my burden is light" (Matthew 11:28–30 NIV).

"Brethren, whatever things are true, whatever things are noble, whatever things are just, whatever things are pure, whatever things are lovely, whatever things are of good report, if there is any virtue and if there is anything praiseworthy—meditate on these things. The things which you learned and received and heard and saw in me, these do, and the God of peace will be with you" (Philippians 4:8–9).

'The glory of this latter temple shall be greater than the former,' says the Lord of hosts. 'And in this place I will give peace,' says the Lord of hosts" (Haggai 2:9).

"The kingdom of God is not eating and drinking, but righteousness and peace and joy in the Holy Spirit" (Romans 14:17).

"The God of peace will crush Satan under your feet shortly. The grace of our Lord Jesus Christ be with you. Amen" (Romans 16:20).

"God was pleased to have all his fullness dwell in him, and through him to reconcile to himself all things, whether things on earth or things in heaven, by making peace through his blood, shed on the cross" (Colossians 1:19–20 NIV).

"Not only that, but all the broken and dislocated pieces of the universe—people and things, animals and atoms—get properly fixed and fit together in vibrant harmonies, all because of his death, his blood that poured down from the cross" (Colossians 1:20 MSG).

"Peace I leave with you, My peace I give to you; not as the world gives do I give to you. Let not your heart be troubled, neither let it be afraid" (John 14:27).

"Then, the same day at evening, being the first day of the week, when the doors were shut where the disciples were assembled, for fear of the Jews, Jesus came and stood in the midst, and said to them, "Peace be with you" (John 20:19).

"Blessed are the peacemakers, for they shall be called sons of God" (Matthew 5:9).

"Seek peace and pursue it" (Psalm 34:14).

"But Jesus was calmly sleeping in the stern, resting on a cushion" (Mark 4:38 TPT).

"Then He arose and rebuked the wind, and said to the sea, 'Peace, be still!' And the wind ceased and there was a great calm" (Mark 4:39).

"Cast all your anxiety on him because he cares for you" (1 Peter 5:7 NIV).

"You will keep him in perfect peace,
Whose mind is stayed on You,
Because he trusts in You" (Isaiah 26:3).

"I will both lie down in peace, and sleep; for You alone, O Lord, make me dwell in safety" (Psalm 4:8).

"He was pierced for our transgressions,
 he was crushed for our iniquities;
the punishment that brought us peace was on him,
 and by his wounds we are healed" (Isaiah 53:5 NIV).

"I sought the Lord, and he answered me; he delivered me from all my fears" (Psalm 34:4 NIV).

"Be still, and know that I am God;
I will be exalted among the nations,
I will be exalted in the earth!" (Psalm 46:10).

"The Lord will give strength to His people;
The Lord will bless His people with peace" (Psalm 29:11).

The Lord is my shepherd;
I shall not want.
He makes me to lie down in green pastures;
He leads me beside the still waters.
He restores my soul;
He leads me in the paths of righteousness
For His name's sake.
Yea, though I walk through the valley of the shadow of death,
I will fear no evil;
For You are with me;
Your rod and Your staff, they comfort me.
You prepare a table before me in the presence of my enemies;
You anoint my head with oil;
My cup runs over.
Surely goodness and mercy shall follow me
All the days of my life;
And I will dwell in the house of the Lord
Forever.
(Psalm 23)

APPENDIX 2

How to Have Peace with God

Having been justified by faith, we have peace with God through our Lord Jesus Christ.
—Romans 5:1

If you made it to this page, and aren't sure of where you'll spend eternity, please keep on reading.

Before you can really live in the peace *of* God, you need to have peace *with* God.

The reality is, your sins have separated you from God. That leaves you in a place of chaos and restlessness. Jesus came to bring you back to God and put you back in order; to give you peace.

The peace of God comes by first making peace with God.

We were all enemies of God and deserving of His wrath and punishment. But the good news is that Christ took what we deserved: "God demonstrates His own love toward us, in that while we were still sinners, Christ died for us" (Romans 5:8).

> But he was pierced for our transgressions,
> he was crushed for our iniquities;
> the punishment that brought us peace was on him,
> and by his wounds we are healed.
>
> —Isaiah 53:5 NIV

God loved us and made a way for us to be forgiven. Jesus died for our sins and to bring us peace. We go from being enemies to beloved sons and daughters. That is peace with God. It's time to repent—turn away from your sins and turn to God. "For the wages of sin is death, but the gift of God is eternal life in Christ Jesus our Lord." (Romans 6:23).

At this very moment, you can receive forgiveness of sins, have a home in heaven for eternity—and most of all, begin a right relationship with God.

Will you receive His free gift?

Will you turn away from your sins and become a follower of Jesus today?

Pray this prayer right now:

> *Lord Jesus,*
>
> *I come to You now. I ask You to forgive me.*
> *I believe You died on the cross for my sins, You were buried, and on the third day You rose again.*
> *Come into my heart.*
> *I make You my Lord and my Savior.*

This day, I turn away from my sins and I receive Your forgiveness.
I put my faith in You and receive Your peace.
I give You my life.
Empower me to live this life for You.

In Jesus' name, amen.

If you prayed this prayer, please let us know! We want to celebrate with you and send you a free gift. Email us at: info@breakerministries.com.

Find a good Bible-believing, Holy Spirit-filled, Jesus-glorifying church to attend. This way, you'll be able to grow and connect with others who share the same faith. The best is yet to come!

APPENDIX 3

Be Filled with the Holy Spirit

"I am going to send you what my Father has promised; but stay in the city until you have been clothed with power from on high."
—Luke 24:49

Some of Jesus' last words before He ascended into heaven were to wait until they were clothed with power from on high. He was speaking of the Holy Spirit that would empower them to be witnesses for Him (Acts 1:8).

Jesus basically said don't go into all the world until you have supernatural power from the Spirit of God. If the disciples who literally walked with Jesus couldn't fulfill the call of God on their lives without power from on high, how much more do we need the Holy Spirit?

The supernatural power of God was normal to the early believers. Healings, miracles, visions, prophecies, the gifts of the Spirit, and the help of angels were all normal. In fact, Jesus said Himself that those who believe in Him would do what He had been doing and even greater works! (John 14:12). They lived lives of righteousness and purity before God.

We need God's help to live like Jesus!

This all comes through the power of the Holy Spirit.

I want to invite you to receive the baptism of the Holy Spirit. To baptize means to be fully immersed in. God wants to clothe you with supernatural power.

One of the signs that you've been clothed and fully immersed in this power is the gift of speaking in tongues. Jesus said it's available to all who believe (Mark 16:17). It's a supernatural language that God gives you that has amazing benefits to your walk with Christ.

If you've never been filled with the Holy Spirit, pray this prayer:

> *Father God,*
>
> *I need Your power. So Jesus, baptize me with the Holy Spirit. Come Holy Spirit and fill me up. Clothe me with power from on high. I receive the gifts of the Spirit and the supernatural nature of God.*
>
> *In Jesus' name, amen.*

Now just let Him fill you.

You may begin speaking in a new language. Just let it flow. Receive power from on high in Jesus' name.

You may begin to see visions, hear the voice of God amplified, or just physically feel God coming upon you. I bless what God is doing in your life, in Jesus' name.

Just wait upon Him and let Him move in your life.

If you prayed this prayer, please let us know! We want to hear how God moved and send you a free gift. Email us at: info@breakerministries.com.

ENDNOTES

---

1 Giving credit where credit is due, I first heard Louie Giglio share this in a sermon around 2003.
2 "G2347 - thlipsis - Strong's Greek Lexicon (kjv)." Blue Letter Bible. Accessed 13 Jan, 2022.
https://www.blueletterbible.org/lexicon/g2347/kjv/tr/0-1/
3 "H7965 - šālôm - Strong's Hebrew Lexicon (kjv)." Blue Letter Bible. Accessed 13 Jan, 2022.
https://www.blueletterbible.org/lexicon/h7965/kjv/wlc/0-1/
4 NET Bible® footnotes on Isaiah 9:6, copyright ©1996-2017 by Biblical Studies Press, L.L.C. http://netbible.com
5 Dictionary.com, "peace", accessed Jan. 13, 2022,
https://www.dictionary.com/browse/peace
6 Dictionary.com, "peace", accessed Jan. 13, 2022,
https://www.dictionary.com/browse/peace
7 Oxford Languages, "humanism", accessed Jan. 13, 2022,
https://www.lexico.com/en/definition/humanism
8 Dictionary.com, "humanism", accessed Jan. 13, 2022,
https://www.dictionary.com/browse/humanism
9 A.W. Tozer, *Knowledge of the Holy* (New York: HarperCollins, 1961), p. 1
10 Julie Winter, *Renew: Breaking Free from Negative Thinking, Anxiety, and Depression* (Pennsylvania: Destiny Image Publishers, Inc., 2017)
[11]11 "G4991 - sōtēria - Strong's Greek Lexicon (kjv)." Blue Letter Bible. Accessed 13 Jan, 2022.
https://www.blueletterbible.org/lexicon/g4991/kjv/tr/0-1/
12 "G4982 - sōzō - Strong's Greek Lexicon (kjv)." Blue Letter Bible. Accessed 13 Jan, 2022.
https://www.blueletterbible.org/lexicon/g4982/kjv/tr/0-1/
13 "G604 - apokatallassō - Strong's Greek Lexicon (kjv)." Blue Letter Bible. Accessed 13 Jan, 2022.
https://www.blueletterbible.org/lexicon/g604/kjv/tr/0-1/
14 "G1517 - eirēnopoieō - Strong's Greek Lexicon (kjv)." Blue Letter Bible. Accessed 13 Jan, 2022.

https://www.blueletterbible.org/lexicon/g1517/kjv/tr/0-1/
15 Dictionary.com, "atonality", accessed Jan. 13, 2022, https://www.dictionary.com/browse/atonality
16 "H7363 - rāḥap̄ - Strong's Hebrew Lexicon (kjv)." Blue Letter Bible. Accessed 13 Jan, 2022. https://www.blueletterbible.org/lexicon/h7363/kjv/wlc/0-1/
17 Craig Groeschel, *Winning the War in Your Mind,* (Michigan: Zondervan, 2021), p. 1, 12
18 Abide in Christ, "Jesus Asleep on a Pillow by C. H. Spurgeon", accessed Jan. 13, 2022, http://www.asermon.com/books/spurgeon-tilhecome-jesusasleep.html
19 "G4623 - siōpaō - Strong's Greek Lexicon (kjv)." Blue Letter Bible. Accessed 13 Jan, 2022. https://www.blueletterbible.org/lexicon/g4623/kjv/tr/0-1/
20 "G5392 - phimoō - Strong's Greek Lexicon (kjv)." Blue Letter Bible. Accessed 13 Jan, 2022. https://www.blueletterbible.org/lexicon/g5392/kjv/tr/0-1/
21 Dictionary.com, "worry", accessed Jan. 13, 2022, https://www.dictionary.com/browse/worry
22 Abide in Christ, "Jesus Asleep on a Pillow by C. H. Spurgeon," accessed Jan. 13, 2022, http://www.asermon.com/books/spurgeon-tilhecome-jesusasleep.html
23 "G2663 - katapausis - Strong's Greek Lexicon (KJV)." Blue Letter Bible. Accessed 13 Jan, 2022. https://www.blueletterbible.org/lexicon/g2663/kjv/tr/0-1/
24 Seth Dahl, "Is it possible not to worry?", accessed Jan. 13, 2022, https://sethdahl.com/blog/2020/3/18/is-it-possible-to-not-worry?rq=worry
25 Abide in Christ, "Jesus Asleep on a Pillow by C. H. Spurgeon", accessed Jan. 13, 2022, http://www.asermon.com/books/spurgeon-tilhecome-jesusasleep.html
26 Bill Scheidler, *The Book of Acts Teacher's Manual* (Church Leadership Resources, 2015), p. 48, http://www.churchleadershipresources.com/curriculum.html

27 History.com editors, "Samurai and Bushido", updated Aug. 21, 2018, accessed Jan. 14, 2022, https://www.history.com/topics/japan/samurai-and-bushido

28 AncientPages.com, "Katana 'Soul Of The Samurai' – Most Famous Japanese Sword With Long Tradition", April 12, 2018, accessed Jan. 14, 2022, https://www.ancientpages.com/2018/04/12/katana-soul-of-the-samurai-most-famous-japanese-sword-with-long-tradition/

29 "G5432 - phroureō - Strong's Greek Lexicon (KJV)." Blue Letter Bible. Accessed 14 Jan, 2022. https://www.blueletterbible.org/lexicon/g5432/kjv/tr/0-1/

30 Dictionary.com, "garrison", accessed Jan. 14, 2022, https://www.dictionary.com/browse/garrison

31 "G342 - anakainōsis - Strong's Greek Lexicon (kjv)." Blue Letter Bible. Accessed 14 Jan, 2022. https://www.blueletterbible.org/lexicon/g342/kjv/tr/0-1/

32 "H7623 - šāḇaḥ - Strong's Hebrew Lexicon (kjv)." Blue Letter Bible. Accessed 14 Jan, 2022. https://www.blueletterbible.org/lexicon/h7623/kjv/wlc/0-1/

33 "G3618 - oikodomeō - Strong's Greek Lexicon (kjv)." Blue Letter Bible. Accessed 14 Jan, 2022. https://www.blueletterbible.org/lexicon/g3618/kjv/tr/0-1/

34 "H6430 - pᵊlištî - Strong's Hebrew Lexicon (kjv)." Blue Letter Bible. Accessed 14 Jan, 2022. https://www.blueletterbible.org/lexicon/h6430/kjv/wlc/0-1/

35 Dictionary.com, "immigrant", accessed Jan. 14, 2022, https://www.dictionary.com/browse/immigrant

36 United Church of Christ Norwell, "Asleep in the Stern," updated Jan. 5, 2022, accessed Jan. 14, 2022, https://www.uccnorwell.org/daily-devotionals-1/e0ct7xe792ayil03ehty7fldtxwu6h

37 "G2091 - hetoimasia - Strong's Greek Lexicon (KJV)." Blue Letter Bible. Accessed 14 Jan, 2022. https://www.blueletterbible.org/lexicon/g2091/kjv/tr/0-1/

38 Dictionary.com, "umpire", accessed Jan. 14, 2022, https://www.dictionary.com/browse/umpire

ABOUT THE AUTHOR

Andrew Hopkins is a prophetic worship leader and a revelatory preacher and teacher. He has a passion for the gospel, revival, equipping the saints, and seeing God move in supernatural ways. He worked at his local church for over a decade in various pastoral positions and currently heads up his own itinerate ministry, Breaker Ministries. He also works at Elisha Revolution with Jerame and Miranda Nelson as worship director and associate revivalist.

Andrew earned a bachelor's degree in Christian Studies in worship from Vision International University. He and his beautiful wife Rochelle have two boys, Hunter and Everett, and live in San Diego, California.

STAY CONNECTED

Website: breakerministries.com
Instagram: @andrewwhopkins
Facebook: @AndrewHopkinsBreaker

Join our email list today and receive a *FREE 7-day devotional* on breakthrough praise and worship called *Expand Your Expression.*

Sign up at www.breakerministries.com.

EXPAND YOUR EXPRESSION

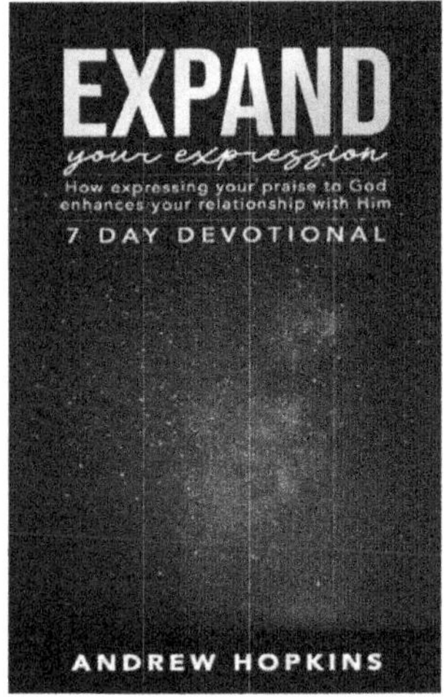

Most Christians want to experience God in a profound way, but when it comes to praise and worship, they're content to let the more "passionate" people fully engage while they stay generally mild in their expression. It's been said that if you do what you've always done, you'll get what you've always got. Specifically in the area of outwardly expressing praise and worship, the Lord wants to push people out of what they've always done so they can discover Him in a fresh way!

Take the 7-day journey into breakthrough and freedom in praise!

Carriers of the Ark

In the Old Testament, the priests carried the Ark of the Covenant on their shoulders, but in the New Testament, the fulfillment of the Ark came to live within the believers—*Christ in you, the hope of glory! (Col. 1:27).*

Many Christians want to have an external demonstration of God's power flowing in their lives yet don't always have the internal fortitude formed through surrender and sacrifice. As a result, many have a hard time sustaining the flow of the anointing, the amount of "kingdom come" is limited, and even their own personal revival is capped.

The world around you needs God's presence, and you were created to carry Him! This book is a training manual on what God wants to form *in you* so you can carry more of Him *upon you!*

We are the modern-day *Carriers of the Ark!*

SEND OUT YOUR ROAR EP

Eight original Andrew Hopkins songs that will provoke passion for Jesus, stir up the Spirit of revival and release encounter with the God of the Breakthrough.

Available at **breakerministries.com**

and all online music stores

Curse Reversed EP

Let Andrew Hopkins lead you into a place of praise and gratitude as you celebrate all that Jesus accomplished for you at the cross and resurrection.

Available at **breakerministries.com**

and all online music stores